Open For You

Paul Bond is an Anglican priest who was involved with church tourism for many years as National Liaison Officer of the Churches Tourism Association – formerly the National Churches Tourism Group.

He worked in the Church of England and the Church in Wales before retiring from parish ministry to the Cotswolds, where he now lives.

Open For You

The Church, the Visitor and the Gospel

Paul Bond

CANTERBURY PRESS

Norwich

Text © Paul Bond 2006
Illustrations © Patricia Bond 2006

First published in 2006 by the Canterbury Press Norwich
(a publishing imprint of Hymns Ancient & Modern Limited,
a registered charity)
9–17 St Alban's Place, London
NI ONX

www.scm-canterburypress.co.uk

British Library Cataloguing in Publication data

A catalogue record for this book is available
from the British Library

ISBN 1-85311-714-5/978-1-85311-714-5

Typeset by Regent Typsesetting, London
Printed and bound by
CPD (Wales) Ltd, Ebbw Vale

Contents

Foreword

In today's church people talk about church buildings as if they were a millstone around our necks and an obstacle to the mission of God. They are seen as the mascots of maintenance rather than the motivators of mission. If you take this view then this book is not for you! Or maybe it is. Here you will find such a positive attitude to church buildings that you will reassess the potential of yours.

Church buildings are not just sermons, but symphonies in stone serenading those with the ears to hear and the eyes to see with the stories of local communities and their discovery of the love of God through all the changing scenes of life.

I love seeing the faces of children who come into Liverpool's Anglican Cathedral for the first time. 'What do you make of it?' 'Cool!' 'Boss!'

I'm intrigued by the strangers who gaze up into the cavernous space as the missionary spirit of God begins to interpret the building to an opening mind and soul, turning the tourist into a pilgrim. What worries me is the indifference of the faithful as we go about our business hardly sparing a prayer for those caught up in this spiritual encounter.

After I confirmed one man I asked him what had led him to faith. He said that when they replaced the wooden west door with one of glass he was able to see inside and pluck up courage to enter in. We forget just how forbidding our closed heavy doors can be.

The story from the Bible that kept coming to mind as I read this book was of Philip meeting the Ethiopian eunuch while he was reading the scriptures on his chariot in the desert. Philip asked him if he understood what he was reading. The Ethiopian rightly objected and replied: 'How can I unless someone explains it to me?' Today's strangers to our familiar buildings need us to come alongside them in the same way to interpret these stones. Philip rose to the challenge and so must we, otherwise people will go on their way with their eyes still closed and their seeking hearts still lost.

There's a spiritual instinct in all of us. It comes alive from time to time. When it does it often drives the person to a church. This book is full of practical suggestions as to how you can engage these latter-day seekers. This book, even partially implemented in a local church, has the potential of turning tourists into pilgrims. Taken seriously this book will convert you from maintenance to mission.

James Jones
Bishop of Liverpool

About this Book

Whether your church building is open every day or only when you are holding a special event, there is a wonderful opportunity to convey something of the love of God to your visitors through the medium of the building itself.

Your building might be little more than a convenient room or it might be a gem of architectural heritage but in either case it is the place where you meet with your friends and with God.

And yet, strange as it may seem, if our visitors do not come to worship, they may never know why the building is so special to us.

How to use this book

The book starts with a challenge, followed by a great deal of encouragement, to see and to seize the opportunity that our church buildings give to convey some understanding of the Christian faith to our visitors.

The guiding principle is that the building, its structure and its furnishings, can communicate the good news of a loving God. Once that idea has been grasped there is no need to follow any particular order: each chapter stands by itself. There is some repetition, which I hope is not too annoying: it is intentional.

There is nothing directive here. Each congregation is encouraged to work out its own scheme, simply using the ideas and examples as a stimulus to action. Everyone can do something: no one should do everything.

At the end of most chapters you are invited to ask yourself some questions. Using these might help you to start on your own programme. It is our heartfelt prayer that you will want to give your visitors, Christian and non-Christian alike, a greater understanding of the Christian faith and an opportunity to draw near to God.

History

A few years ago I became the National Liaison Officer of the National Churches Tourism Group (now the Churches Tourism Association). What attracted me to NCTG was the idea of helping thousands of churches to relate the gospel to those who visit churches outside the times designated for worship.

I subsequently asked three friends from NCTG to form a group which we called BMR – (church) buildings as a mission resource. They were Jeff Bonser, Brian Godfrey and Alan Pyke, each of whom, in their own work, had already evidenced the same passion to communicate the good news of God's love. This book is the outcome of our co-operation, a few meetings and hundreds of e-mails. Brian has written the Churchyard chapter and Alan has assembled the extensive resource list, although we are all responsible for errors and omissions.

Gratitude

We have consulted with a great number of people. None of them is mentioned by name within the book although the information some supplied has reached the book under the name of their church. Others commented at large on the text. These included Linda Allcock, Gillian Allison, Keith Barltrop, Stuart Bell, Mark Bryant, Paul Dicken, John Drane, David Spriggs, Stephen Platten and Ro Willoughby. I should also mention Herb and Hermione for their comments on the cartoons and the illustrator, my wife Patricia, who will now, doubtless, be in demand to enliven otherwise dull texts. Our expenses have been met by the Christian Initiative Trust to whom we are pleased to donate the royalties from the sale of this book. To all of these friends and to many others who have offered help, shown interest and supported us in prayer, I offer our grateful thanks.

Paul Bond
2006

1

The Best Kept Secret

We found a church. It was fronting two roads in suburban Birmingham but what sort of church was it? It was Saturday and we were looking for somewhere to worship on Sunday. It wasn't that we couldn't find the notice board; it just didn't exist. The door was locked.

Passing through a seemingly deserted village in Oxfordshire we saw a plain but clear sign by the roadside: the sort that is found outside a pub. It simply said, 'Open for You'. It wasn't a pub. It was a church – and it was Wednesday.

As we have travelled we have found countless open churches in town and country. Thank you. We have entered and enjoyed our visits. If we happened to meet one of the congregation we noticed their pride and were warmed by their welcome. If no one was there we still found a welcome and evidence of love and care – often much more than the common entry in the visitors' book: 'lovely, so peaceful'.

But we have rarely discovered anything about the Christian faith.

Why is that? If we visit a silk factory we learn much about the process of producing silken goods. If we visit a railway museum we read about the heroes of the age of steam. If we visit a laboratory we are introduced to the techniques and skills that are employed. Everywhere we visit, people want to share their knowledge and enthusiasm with us! We hope that this book will help you to use your church buildings to share your faith with your visitors.

Why do people visit churches?

It might seem peculiar to say that many visitors are little more than passers-by: for most the visit to our church is not the prime object of their journey. Often it is a secondary activity when they are in the neighbourhood or simply because they saw the church, even from some distance, and thought they would have a look. Sometimes there is a spiritual quest. Richard Askew in *From Strangers to Pilgrims* describes how God spoke to Susan Howatch through the beauty of Salisbury Cathedral.

> Round and round the Cathedral I walked . . . Eventually I began to go inside for a few minutes each day not to pray, because I did not know how, but simply to be and to hope that one day I might become a person more at peace with myself . . . become the person, whoever it was, that I was supposed to be. That . . . describes the beginning of my religious conversion.

She goes on to give thanks for 'radiant, ravishing Salisbury where I received not only new life but – by the grace of Our Lord Jesus Christ – new life in abundance.'

In addition there are visitors from close-by; there are those who are seeking graves of long-deceased ancestors and others who are particularly interested in a treasure in your building. Some may be organised special interest groups of, say, bell-ringers or brass-rubbers and others are children on a school project. One special interest group that it is easy to overlook are those who come for celebrations such as thanksgivings, baptisms, dedications, confirmations, weddings and funerals. The sharing of faith with them – other than what happens in the service itself – will need an approach different from that taken with other visitors. Those who visit for a special service tend to walk in, sit down and at the end of the service get up and leave together.

Huge numbers of people visit churches in town and village, in city and countryside, by accident or on purpose, entering into cathedral, meeting house, chapel or church. Possibly more people visit churches than all other attractions added together, many of which are heavily advertised. In one way that is not surprising as such a high proportion of our heritage is to be found in churches. More than 8,000 have been receiving visitors for over 500 years. Wherever your church is and whatever it is like, you will have visitors, providing your doors are open. How many come? A study in Lincolnshire found that only about 10 per cent of visitors put their name in the visitors' book, so your visitor numbers may be much greater than you thought.

The one consistent fact to note about each of the 20 million or so visitors to churches every year is that they have chosen to go at a time that suits them and they have gone for their own purposes – even to shelter from the rain –

rather than choosing to attend at a time of worship. Those joining in worship hear the good news of the love of God and the purpose of life, they experience the fellowship of believers, they confess their sins, they express their praise and thanksgiving, they partake of a divine mystery and, hopefully, they are spiritually satisfied or challenged. What will you offer to those who come at times of their own choosing? How will you share the good news of God? It is true that over the past 150 years the numbers who attend church services have been declining yet many would say that interest in spiritual matters of all kinds seems greater than ever. More visitors could come to your church during the week than are ever seen on Sundays.

More visitors could come to your church during the week than are ever seen on Sundays.

Is there a risk in having an open church?

Risk assessment is something that Jesus knew all about. A biblical example is that of the good shepherd (John 10.10). The shepherd's responsibility involved risk taking and risk management: he was alert to the danger and took appropriate measures. In seeming contrast to that parable, Jesus actually sent out 70 disciples with no protection and no resources although surely not before making a sound judgement about the level of the risk. If the church is left open and without someone in attendance, what is the level of risk and how should it be managed?

The Ecclesiastical Insurance Group writes in its *Guidance Notes on Church Security* that a church should be left open during the day. The visitors' book often provides another reason. 'Thank you for having this church open' could be the testimony of someone whose life has been changed because you took the risk. To be fair, it is possible that the same remark could express the gratitude of someone who left with your candlesticks!

Good advice for the care of churches is available and should be followed. An excellent starting point is Nick Tolson's *Places of Worship Security Manual*. Obviously police and insurance companies recommend certain general precautions and they will give specific advice to anyone who asks. Beyond that they advise sound common sense and an awareness that the criminally motivated and the vandal are always with us.

There are thousands of churches open during the day in town and country. If yours is closed please think again. Does your church have features so distinctive as to dictate the necessity of a fortress mentality? Many others face similar risks and yet they have decided to stay open. Why is this?

They will say they believe that God is hospitable and welcoming and they think that a locked door denies this truth. They consider it a great privilege to have been appointed stewards of a priceless possession and think that others should be able to enjoy the beauty and the sacred space that their building affords. But others have gone further. They have realised that in various ways the building itself can be used to declare boldly, as well as disclose gently, the God whom they worship. It is in this place where God is worshipped that Christian faith can be properly, willingly and joyfully shared with others.

There is no doubt that this is a difficult issue. Those with the most legitimate concerns perhaps relate to churches in the unobserved deep countryside and those in the anonymous inner city. There is also no doubt as to who will

have to attend to the consequences of any untoward behaviour and those who have such responsibility are properly concerned to ensure the building is in an appropriate condition for those who wish to worship. Nevertheless, could one pertinent question be raised on the basis of Jesus' story of the man who protected what was entrusted to him, rather than using it in the best possible way? (The story of the talents in Matthew 25.24.) The question is this: is there a harvest that the Lord might reap from an open church that would be denied him if the church were locked? If, however, you have a locked church and, for the love of God, you are now prepared to consider opening it, make your action plan and review it in six months' time. Use all your wisdom and remember that the Lord praised the streetwise in the parable of the dishonest manager in Luke 16.8.

Some questions to consider

- What do visitors like about our church?

- Is being open a risk worth taking? How can we assess and manage the risk?

- How can we best demonstrate that God is welcoming and hospitable?

- Can we open every day without hosts? If not, how do we recruit and train hosts?

- How can we help our visitors discover the love of God?

- How could we reach those who go to other visitor attractions in our area?

2

An Accessible Faith

We don't do evangelism

When the interviewer asked Tony Blair about God, his Director of Communications, Alistair Campbell, interrupted to say, 'We don't do God'. Similarly, if talking about God is mentioned in Church, many people are inclined to think, 'We don't do evangelism!' Don't worry; this book will simply help you to use your building to share your faith. We sometimes say our faith is private but it need not be absolutely secret and hidden from others.

Your church might be different but it is true of most churches that if visitors enter during the week without knowing God they leave without knowing God. If they enter without knowing God loves them, they leave without knowing God loves them. If they enter without knowing there is good news, they leave without knowing there is good news. If they enter with a host of spiritual questions they find few answers.

It is true of most churches that if visitors enter during the week without knowing God they leave without knowing God.

The architecture, the windows, the carvings, the memorials, the pictures, the furnishings and stained glass are all interpreted. We are informed by printed guide or bat board, by free handout or framed notice, about the period and place of creation, the style and artistic merit, the craftsman and the patron. Sometimes we are given access to local history and even legends but rarely is there any sort of faith interpretation of anything in the building or its contents.

Is there no Christian story to tell? Why is there no explanation of Christian faith? Hopefully the

Spirit of God ministered to people in your congregation this very week. Surely, that was more important to you than the furnishings, the fabrics and the other features of the building? God has more for your visitor than the building itself can offer.

You may have decided long ago – or reading this you may decide now – to be hospitable. You are pleased that people come in during the week and perhaps come in without any invitation other than an open door. You know the church is not a museum: you know it houses the local community of faith. It is the church (building) in which the Church (people) meet to worship the living God. What will your visitor learn about the living God?

Peter Baelz, Dean of Durham until 1988, is quoted by Richard Askew in *From Strangers to Pilgrims*:

> Historic churches suffer from two handicaps: that a stone building may not be conducive to communicating a message that is, at its heart, about people, or rather a Person; and that old buildings tend to suggest that the Christian message also belongs to the past.

G. K. Chesterton bemoaned the fact that it had taken him years of visits to foreign places of religion and local places of philosophy to find a simple Christian faith that he might have found in his local parish church. 'If only', as they say!

The beautiful church of St Mary, in one of our old market towns, is a delight to visit. Attractively presented, there is a well-stocked bookstall, welcome leaflets for visitors in several languages and attentive, smiling hosts. 'What is this building for?' asked a visitor. There followed an awkward silence. Whatever instruction the hosts received it had not covered that question!

Please, as an experiment, visit your own church. Work on the assumption that you are neither the most well-informed and learned person of your generation, nor the world's most brilliant detective, and that there is no resident evangelist. Better still, ask a non-Christian friend to do the survey. Do not stay longer than most visitors.

Based solely on your visit, what do you now know about the Christian faith? You may not have learned much, but it doesn't have to be like that. This book has been written to help you realise how easy it would be for you to use your church building to share your Christian faith.

For those who feel that they do not want to tell people too much but would rather their visitors simply had an experience of God, here is something to consider. Imagine a caller finds no one at home and leaves a visiting card. Or only a note scribbled on a piece of scrap paper that was handy. At least you know who called. Now in the kingdom of God everything is back to front or upside down or inside out! The first shall be last and all that. How wonderful if your visitor, as well as leaving their name in the book supplied, was able to leave with some identification of the person they had visited! A sort of reverse visiting card. When your visitor has had a wonderful experience, surely it would be good to know something about the God who gave that experience – and who has so much more to offer.

The possibilities

European law is greatly concerned with ease of access to public buildings. It may be a nuisance, it may be difficult to implement and it might come as an exceedingly irritating burden on those who have not cared too much whether wheelchair users can get through the door or whether those with poor eyesight can read the small print. From a Christian perspective, however, who could refuse people suffering from certain handicaps the good things that others receive?

Imagine, though, that a new law required that the Christian faith itself must be made accessible to every visitor to your church. How would your church fare? Of course there would be nothing to force anyone to visit and nothing to dictate what they choose to believe – but it would require you to be a little more open about the reason the church is there.

How would you set about making the good news of God more accessible? This will depend on you and on how you think or feel about your faith or how you experience it. There is no single answer. Each church is different and every person understands or expresses their faith in a way that fits their own temperament. Not only that, but each visitor is also different and will see, feel, think and understand in a way that is natural to them. There is no right way to convey the good news. You can try out your own ideas and ask others for their opinions, and from time to time even ask your visitors how they 'read' what you have offered. It is your building and it is your choice. The point of this book is to stimulate, encourage and assist you to make your faith relevant to other people through the use of your church building.

Make your faith relevant to other people through the use of your church building.

The very shape and plan of your church, the ornaments and furnishings, the windows and pictures, the banners and notice boards, the books and displays, and anything left around from the last time of worship will have a relevance to your faith and can therefore be used to communicate it to others.

Much more that can help you achieve your objective will be covered in the chapters that lie ahead. But it would not matter if you jumped now to Chapter 5 for a general introduction to ways of disclosing the Christian meaning of the building and its furnishings. Chapter 11 has further examples of the way some congregations have decided to share their faith through the building. In some ways Chapter 4 is the most revolutionary; the first part in particular, as it deals with your new congregation; the one that visits throughout the week. If many words send you to sleep, why not pick your way through the book by using the cartoons or the displayed quotations? Let the book give you some ideas and then work out your own scheme. Keep thinking, praying, observing and taking notice of the reactions of your visitors.

To interpret everything in terms of faith would be excessive; one area of the church could be highlighted at one time and another later. The seasons of the year or the Church calendar might suggest a particular approach. References to the local community and to the world at large on notices and posters will tell your visitor about your Christian outlook and reveal what is important to you in your life of faith. Look around, consider what each item means in terms of Christian faith and decide whether it could be used in some way to offer insights to your visitors.

Before proceeding, a word of caution is appropriate. Not about the type of your activity but against any assumption that your visitors are familiar with the Christian faith. It may surprise you that 40 per cent of your visitors will rarely, if ever, attend any sort of worship in church and a higher percentage will probably have little knowledge of Christianity. Ours is no longer a Christian society. There was a time when most people living in the UK would be offended if it was suggested that they were not Christian but in the last 50 years this situation has almost been reversed. The teaching of Christianity is still part of the school curriculum and, legally, should form the major input in Religious Studies. Even so, faith itself is much less likely to be caught than it possibly was in days past, as there are now so few Christian teachers. In addition, schools are not bound into the local community as they once were and the teaching of Christianity might never be related to the local Church or church building.

"WHAT DO YOU BELIEVE?"

"ANYTHING I PLEASE - THIS IS A POST MODERNIST SOCIETY"

Please do not patronise your visitors but do be aware that many of them are not familiar with the Christian faith.

Some questions to consider

- Can we visit our own church to find what it reveals about God's love?

- Why do we go to Church? Can we share the good things we receive?

- Was Dean Baelz right? How could we use our building to advantage?

- Steps, poor lighting and heavy doors are hazardous. Can access be improved?

- Some visitors know little of Christianity. How will that affect what we do?

- If we sometimes have hosts, how can we help them share their faith with visitors?

3

Practise hospitality

It's your home

There are churches where a kettle, tea and milk are left out to enable visitors to have a cuppa. That might not be a good idea for you but do think about what your visitors will find. In some churches – but not yours – they will find dog-eared papers relating to an event that took place last year, or a notice board

that was covered with green baize by Mrs Humphries who died 20 years ago. Could the faded fabric be a sort of memorial to her memory? Regrettably your visitor might not unreasonably conclude that the board is tatty.

It is unfortunate that some people who like their own home to be clean and tidy, warm, well lit and comfortable are not nearly so concerned about their church. It is not that everything has to be smart or new; indeed most treasures will be old and not necessarily in the best condition. But guests in our homes are well cared for and visitors to our church should surely be afforded equal courtesy. If you are an animal lover you might think it would be good to have a water bowl in the church porch for your visitor's dog – just as you do at home for your own dog.

If you go to church every week to meditate on the threadbare flags that hang from the roof – or the strobe lighting if your building is more modern; if you sit wondering at the skill of the craftsmen who created the pulpit – or the flair of the pimple-faced youngster who created the PowerPoint presentation; then these are the first things you might want to share but, hopefully, that is a most unlikely scenario, indeed it is a ridiculous suggestion.

You go to church because what is said and done is very special; because it provides a centre for your life; because it puts right and puts into perspective what happened last week and prepares you for next week. You may not be very good at talking about these things but they are important to you. They can be shared; allow the building to share them; use the building to share them with the visitor you have invited to enter your spiritual home. Do you not think that would be real hospitality?

Signs of welcome

As mentioned in Chapter 1, many of your visitors will not have planned to be with you. Knowing that visitors are often happy to make a diversion or willing to add an extra location to the day's itinerary are very good reasons to signpost your church from as far away as possible. If this suggestion sounds rather odd for a town church you might reflect that many town and city churches do have signs in the adjoining streets and they are often just as necessary as ones placed at a greater distance in the countryside. Large or well-known buildings may wish to be signposted even from a motorway but for most churches more local signing will do. Some signposting comes at a price but elsewhere it is free. The Resources section will point you to the government's website. The rules have changed recently so it is worth checking them.

Once you get on your own church land the decisions are mainly yours, although check with the local authority first. If you are aiming at the motorist do ensure that the sign is large enough to be read at the normal traffic speed. If you feel God is hospitable and that it is a privilege and joy to invite people in, welcome them from as great a distance as possible and sensible, and certainly before they have parked or walked up a long drive, only to find that the church door is locked. If a car parking facility can be indicated, that would be an added bonus; especially in a crowded town with many parking restrictions. Would you consider reviewing any notices prohibiting parking on church land? Do gates that are opened a dozen times a year for a hearse need to be a permanent no-go area?

> *If you feel God is hospitable and that it is a privilege and joy to invite people in, welcome them.*

Some church surroundings suffer a great deal of abuse by users of hypo-
dermic syringes and other adjuncts of a modern lifestyle: for them the outside of the building is indeed hospitable because of its dark recesses or lack
of passers-by. Even in those situations, some of our brothers and sisters in
Christ are able to move in alongside and offer real love. This is not within
the ability or skill of most but if you believe in a God who transforms and a
God who rescues, could you invite those people in from time to time to meet
a Christian street-worker?

Having devised ways to attract visitors they will, before long, be piling
through your door – at which point the visit could end unhappily. The caveats
within the Discrimination Act will mean that the entrance to many churches
will continue to present dangers to the unwary. A dark interior accessed by
unlit steps might, to add the comic to the gravely serious, provide an early
confrontation with a font by someone who had no wish to undergo an initiation ceremony.

If warnings are necessary, ensure they are clear and very difficult to miss. It may even be advisable to display an official hazard sign as used in other public buildings.

Having referred to the potential hazards in the church, consider what sort of earlier welcome there should be as visitors approach the church or in the porch or on the door itself. Some will wish to have free standing boards. These usually have a permanent painted message. Fixed boards may be equally permanent in their message but others are domestic bill boards on which the message can be changed. The welcome may be by poem, picture or text. Permanent sign-writing needs to be of the highest quality but the standard of temporary posters need not be so exacting and there may be members of the local community willing and able to produce them.

St Mary's, Lower Slaughter has a welcome board that can be seen from the road. The heading is simply, 'Welcome to St Mary's Church' below which there are a few lines:

> May you be at home here
> For this is the place where the love of God is made known.
> Bring him your needs
> Especially for his forgiveness and his power.
> And pray for the needs of the world.

That is good but its distinction lies in the welcome. It reads in English, 'welcome to this house of God', and this is repeated in twenty-six languages for the benefit of visitors from far and wide. To replicate that could be a challenge to some town churches that have more than that number of languages even within their own catchment area.

Christians believe that Jesus is the light of the world. He exhorted his disciples to shine, yet for various reasons the house in which we worship him is often dark and this situation is made worse by the lack of bright daylight through much of the year. A timed switch is easy to fit but two other things are needed to make it effective. Firstly your visitor needs to be told where the switch is and be invited to use it and that notice will need to be outside a dark interior. Secondly the timing needs to be set with the duration of your visitor's stay in mind.

Lights switched by some electronic means are more suitable. Better still the church that leaves lights on, with a request not to switch them off. Long-life, low-wattage bulbs are appropriate for that church. It is also possible to install economical low-voltage halogen spotlights to highlight features or texts.

Would you think of having music for your visitor? An organist may some-times practise or a group have a rehearsal but most of the time there will simply be silence. Silence will be appreciated by some visitors but most would not be upset by quiet and light music. Research by the National Churches Tourism Group showed that many people would positively welcome it. The style and size of building may influence what music is used. A music stand with a card, 'the music now playing ...' would be a nice touch. A CD player set on loop could be located out of the reach of interfering or acquisitive fingers.

For a building open to the public – and for our own congregation – the common lack of toilets is seemingly a dereliction of the duty of a good host.

Even Westminster Abbey has no loos but there are uniformed marshals to point visitors to a public toilet across the road. If there are public toilets close by your church or your local Publican will allow his facilities to be used, will you provide a notice to that effect?

Discrimination

Our daily actions and options are increasingly conditioned by legislation. Some requirements might induce mild apoplexy but it is interesting that good behaviour and social expectation can be enhanced by law. The speed limit of 30 mph in a built-up area might originally have been an arbitrary figure but it has acquired a moral obligation. Driving at excessive speeds clearly demonstrates a disregard for the well-being of others.

"HE WOULD LIKE TO GO FASTER"

"SHE CAN'T MANAGE MORE THAN 3 MPH"

The Disability Discrimination Act 1995 imposes a legal duty on Churches to be inclusive and accessible to disabled people. Whereas many Church members might be aggrieved at the cost of implementing such legislation, few would be prepared to say, 'Jesus doesn't want disabled people to be members of our worshipping community.' This book is not primarily considering the activity of the Church at worship but the law intends that the worshipping community and the Monday to Saturday congregation of visitors should be equal beneficiaries of the heritage on offer. Physical barriers to access should have been adjusted by October 2004 yet there was still much work still to be done when that date had passed. There are, of course, anomalies; for instance nothing in the Act enforces the provision of a toilet, which might please the Treasurers of both small country churches and Westminster Abbey. Does any of this have to do with communicating the gospel to your visitor? Nothing at all in respect of the legal detail but everything as far as love and care is concerned.

Through the Roof, a Christian organisation that addresses questions of disability, has written:

> It is people's attitudes that make a real difference – if a Church genuinely wants to be inclusive of disabled people, it will give thought to finding a way around any practical difficulties. Churches who see disabled people as important and precious to God will want to go further than the Act requires, to enable those disabled people to be fully included in all aspects of Church life.

The Resources section suggests where to look for technical guidance but to be practical why not invite a few people from an organisation serving blind and mobility impaired people to visit with some of their members? Listening and taking notice of their and their helpers' advice and comments will immediately establish a good relationship that can be built on. This exercise might bear fruit within your own congregation if it reminds them that Jesus regularly ministered to those who suffered great physical difficulties. Unfortunately many Churches have never had anyone within their congregation suffering from a serious disability, other than that caused by old age.

Few would be prepared to say, 'Jesus doesn't want disabled people to be members of our worshipping community.'

It would be very good if everything provided in print could also be available in large print – indeed one day the law may require it. As most leaflets are now produced locally there can be no difficulty in using the same text to print a larger edition. To say that it would be sensible to place a small notice about this on the welcome table might raise a laugh; let it be a small notice with a heading that boldly proclaims, 'Large Print'. Production in Braille is a different matter, for which specialist equipment is needed. What could be provided is an audio cassette – mentioned briefly in Chapter 5.

Some questions to consider

- Our visitors would be amazed to be offered refreshments. Could we do this?

- Could we improve external notice boards inviting and welcoming visitors?

- Is entry to our church easy and without hazards? How could it be improved?

- How can we prepare a welcome for our visitors that will put a smile on their faces?

- Could we examine our lighting and the cost of electronic or mechanical controls?

- Could sensory provision be made for visitors with sight and hearing disabilities?

4

Adapting to Visitors

Monday to Saturday Church

Entering church on a Sunday – or on a Saturday evening if that is when your main service takes place – is very special. It might be very quiet and reverent or it might be a noisy hubbub. Churches are different and people are different and we make our own choices. Some might even devotedly and conscientiously stay with one congregation when they would really prefer another

"IT'S OPEN ALL HOURS"

"BUT ONLY WHEN THEY TELL YOU ON SUNDAYS"

style but whatever our reactions, we are moved; we are again with people we know and trust, we have a common identity, we take our place and look forward to worship. And then we leave and not many will enter the building again until the same experience is repeated the following week.

How very different it is for those who come during the week. The church (building) is not prepared for an event, an act of corporate worship. There is no immediate welcome of a people gathered in expectancy.

> *It is now a Monday to Saturday congregation. People are coming to your church: not for corporate worship but to enjoy the building.*

It is now a Monday to Saturday congregation. People are coming to your church: not for corporate worship but to enjoy the building which you have kept open for them. Remember that more people might enter during the week than on Sunday and that with a little effort the church can be made ready to welcome them. Can you care for those you will not see, prepare for them, and treat them as another, albeit different, congregation?

Canon George Hall of Sandringham talked of two families – one that gathered to worship on a Sunday, the other that came during the week. What an opportunity to share the good news of Jesus.

Why not willingly seize such an evident opportunity? Indeed, some might go further and even seek to provide some sort of pastoral care.

In most situations the building will have to speak for itself. Not in the sense of 'the stones cry out', although for some visitors they might, but in the sense that the building does not have to be an empty shell or a museum or a place with no purpose until the next event. The building can, with a minimum of effort, be reordered into the configuration of a Monday to Saturday church. Admittedly this will have to be a simple operation otherwise there will not be the necessary enthusiasm on the home front. The weekly reordering is likely to be the responsibility of a small group although the idea of welcome will hopefully be owned by the whole congregation.

There is no limit to new possibilities. Let those given in this book stimulate you to think of ideas that are appropriate for your own church and to the way in which you would like to tell others of what is special to you.

A warm welcome

It may seem a contradiction to talk of a warm welcome if there is no one from the congregation to offer a greeting. This book is written on the basis that the building is not hosted but so much the better if it is: everything mentioned here still applies. Training for a 'ministry of welcome' can be by an officially approved course followed by accreditation – further details are in Chapter 12 – or by local arrangements. The Diocese of St Albans, for instance, has listed reasons why a parish may wish to consider offering such a ministry. Two of their points apply equally to an unhosted church. They are, firstly, the challenge to portray the Church as living faith rather than dead history and, secondly, the opportunity it gives to present the gospel to a 'largely unchurched population'.

To portray the Church as living faith rather than dead history.

Let there be an attractive and significant welcome table for the Monday to Saturday congregation. Indeed many churches have a welcome table on a Sunday but during the week it could have a different purpose. Why not display a little bowl of flowers – fresh throughout the week – and a not-to-be missed sign saying, 'we are glad you are visiting Oxshead Baptist' or something similar, to give your visitor a good feeling?

A real part of welcome is making your visitor feel comfortable. As a 9 year old I remember dragging on my father's arm imploring him to leave the overpowering – and dirty, dark and dismal – abbey that we were visiting. 'Let's get out of here before we are caught up in something' has been recorded in the family archives. Churches, and certainly that abbey, are now, thankfully, much brighter and few will wish to leave through fear.

It is your home but you are not there. How would you like to be welcomed in similar circumstances? A 'goody bag' is usually presented at the end of a party but might you give your visitor something at the outset? A notice on the welcome table could say, 'When you have signed our visitors' book please take a bookmark to remind you of your visit to St Agatha's on the Marsh'. It's amazing how much information can go on a small card. There could be a quotation from the Bible, a mention of something historic and a prayer. And if the adults are to get a card or a bookmark, what will you offer to your younger visitors?

Knowing what to see and, depending on the size of the building, in which direction to go, is one comfort factor. There may well be written guides giving directions and there could be another welcome sign at the crossing, or the chancel steps, or in the main aisle. This will again be a Monday to Saturday feature which will need to be put out ready for Monday and which you may have to move more than once during the week.

> Welcome! We hope you will enjoy your visit. This ancient church has stood here for 600 years and week by week Christians have come together to worship God and still do. That community extending over the centuries has left much for us to appreciate. Please take time to soak up some of the history. We would also invite you to be still for a little while. We are offered the opportunity to meet with God in prayer. Jesus has said that if we believe and trust in him he will give us the power we need for life.

There was someone here

When visitors enter a church they have not arranged to meet the community that uses the building on a weekly basis. Indeed they may not realise that there is a worshipping community. A visitor to Westminster Abbey asked whether services were ever held there – not having read the free leaflet which says clearly:

> Above all, the Abbey is a living Church – a place for Christian worship. Each hour, for a minute or so, we pause to pray. You are invited to join in – or you might prefer to simply pause for some moments of quiet reflection.

There follows an invitation to return for the daily worship. Whether or not your visitors receive such an invitation, the faith we want to share is an extension of what the congregation does in its worship. You might think it appropriate, therefore, to make as many links as possible between your visitor and the worshipping community.

It follows that it might be a good idea to attempt to illustrate what happens in worship. In the church at Sandringham, mentioned earlier, the altar is laid during the week as prepared for the Communion service. In a smaller church and probably at the other end of the building, the children may have been learning about Jesus. Leave the evidence!

"THEY HAD A GOOD TIME YESTERDAY"

" I DIDN'T EXPECT MISS SMITH TO STILL BE HERE"

The importance of lighting was mentioned in Chapter 3. Music is not important in the same way but many people say that it helps to bring the building alive. What sort of music is a matter of taste; although as it would need to be consistently fairly soft, the organ might not be the best instrument. Using simple sensors, music can be switched on with the lights.

Display boards can be visitor focused – and if so, might therefore need putting away every week. A series of boards, dressed on both sides, could very effectively trace the history of the local Church and community on one side and the history of the faith of that community and its worldwide connections on the other. Working for others in the name of the Lord, whether in the local community or abroad, can be a powerful testimony to the love of God. There needs to be a conscious difference in the material and the display designed for your visitor's benefit and that for domestic use, which will be more of an expression of fellowship within the congregation. It is worth emphasising that everything you do in your Monday to Saturday church is to encourage and enable your visitor to engage with Christian faith – something which may be part and parcel of your own life but different or even new for your visitor.

"AND IF THEY PASS THAT PILLAR?"

"THEY GET A FULL SERMON"

Some visitors may be on holiday in your area, others will be local, and some of the locals may be frequent visitors. How will you invite them to join with you in worship? Obviously the minimum is to indicate the service times but do think about it from their angle. What sort of service is it? What demands will be made of a newcomer who is not used to worship? For instance, is the service family friendly, is there any provision for children, how long does it last? To avoid embarrassment, does the notice say that an offering is received at all services? – if that is suitable wording.

Although the floor area of many churches is much greater than that used by the weekly congregation it is often full of pews and therefore not available for

exhibitions, book stalls or even a welcome table. And the pews are not a very comfortable place for travellers to rest for a while. Where such a dedicated area can be set aside, a couple of sofas might be greatly appreciated. And the coffee table – whether or not the beverage is available – is a good place to indicate God's concern for the world by the display of magazines produced by mission societies working both at home and abroad. Check that the magazines are not years out of date. The diocesan newspaper or national Church newspaper and the Church or community magazine might also be there; they should certainly be available somewhere. Will you invite your visitor to take a free copy, even if members of the congregation have to pay for their own copies?

Hopefully your visitor will have had an enjoyable and educative experience and will also have been offered various insights into the good news that the church was built to proclaim. There is much more in the rest of this book about how this might be achieved.

Hopefully your visitor might have become well aware of the activity of the unseen congregation and therefore would not be surprised to see, perhaps close to the exit, the Church aims or mission statement, which are likely to express clear intentions of Christian purpose. There are some comments on mission statements at the end of Chapter 9.

Also, close to the door, there will be the receptacle that a high percentage of visitors wish to see – the place for their gift. You might consider it more appropriate to express thanks for what is donated rather than making an appeal. If it is true for your church, a simple statement that the building is not supported by civic grants or government funds may be worthwhile as many people think the Church – especially the Church of England – is state owned.

You gave a friendly welcome, so why not offer a friendly farewell? 'Thank you for spending time with us. We hope you will come again.' Perhaps even finishing with, 'God be with you as you journey.'

Some questions to consider

- A Monday to Saturday congregation – a radical idea; can we think about it?

- What would we have to put in place that would be good for our new congregation?

- How will we make visiting children aware that they too are welcomed and valued?

- What would it take to design a 'Welcome visitor' area?

- Last Sunday we met with God here – how can we help our visitors to meet him?

- How could we make a link between our visitors and our Sunday congregation?

5

Why is it There, What is it For?

Large, ancient, interesting

Even the smallest church building has a plot larger than most houses, and it stands by itself. Frequently the church is large and may well have a spire or tower that can be seen from some distance. Many are ancient and, being different from other buildings and open for inspection, they attract the curious, the devout, and the knowledgeable. As joked before people may even enter to avoid the rain; seldom do they enter to get warm! Other visitors have a spiritual attraction and are sensitive even to the stonework which seems to have absorbed centuries of prayer; still others find that their trained or untrained eye is satisfied or impressed by the space, the proportions, the craftsmanship, and the sheer beauty of a building that was designed to lift eye and heart to a higher plane. Previous chapters have suggested how your visitors may be made to feel welcome. This chapter encourages you to tell your visitor what happens in your church and why, by referring to the objects and furnishings that are used in your weekly worship. This is not a new idea but few seem to practise it.

Visitors are satisfied by the space, the proportions, the craftsmanship, and the sheer beauty of a building that was designed to lift eye and heart to a higher plane.

A report by the Church Heritage Forum in May 2003 understood this:

The Good News of the Kingdom could be proclaimed by explaining how the buildings and their furnishings and contents tell the story of what God has done in Jesus.

Before thinking of the ways in which these furnishings are used to express your Christian faith do remember two things. Firstly, the gospel, which is so precious to you, was not assimilated in one walk around a church. Nor will it be by your visitors. You are not a museum curator expected to annotate every piece in great detail. The more references there are, the more subtly they will need to be prepared: for example, printing on clear glass at a point near to its related object is barely noticeable from a distance, whereas notices on white card stand out like entries in an art competition. Secondly, although detailed references to the intricacies of your worship will probably find no point of contact with your visitor it may be that there is an object or an action related to your worship that would be stimulating. Something that referred to, say, stress at the workplace or the pressures of family life could be useful. Your visitor might find that good news indeed.

For instance, the idea of forgiveness or the sharing of the peace or the distribution of the bread or the singing of a love song – from, say, Charles Wesley or Graham Kendrick, depending on your taste – might resonate with the situation in a visitor's own life. How might you do this? Why not write some cards dealing with different issues? One could be headed, 'Ever been in love?' with words below such as:

Many might know that Christians talk about loving God and yet find it offensive to think of singing a love song to God. But that is just what we do. Here is part of a hymn we sing, written 150 years ago!

> Take my love, my Lord, I pour
> at thy feet its treasure store;
> take myself, and I will be
> ever, only, all, for Thee.

Weekly worship

As you work through the items that follow, try to picture them in use. Recollect any thoughts and feelings they have stirred in you. Tell your visitors about them in a way that will catch both eye and imagination. See Chapter 11 for further examples of the ways you can do this

Have a limited number of interpretations displayed at any one time.

The way in which such aids to understanding are displayed will vary. You will want to do what is suitable – which will be influenced by the nature and style of your own church building. One thing is certain: everything should be of a good standard. If anything is to be fixed or permanent it may need permission from an authority that has responsibility for maintaining building and furnishing quality. You may plan the provision you make for your visitors, deciding, for instance, to have a limited number of interpretations displayed at any one time and varying them month by month. Such constant attention will ensure that they stay fresh.

The pulpit

Humour may be an indispensable part of a full humanity and we know all about the pulpit being six feet above contradiction but our task here is more joyful than funny; it is a serious attempt to tell of a loving God.

What should be said about the pulpit? What is it for? If it is no longer used can you say why not? The church guide of a Hampshire parish may tell us, 'The Jacobean pulpit of carved oak is very fine. From this pulpit, it is said, Master Holmes, the minister, was arrested during his sermon by Cromwellian soldiers and taken to Farnham Castle,' but what of the hundreds who, from that same pulpit, have been told of a God who loves them, who knows their failings and shortcomings and who has offered them a new life and a greater hope? If good news is preached from your pulpit, rejoice, and rejoice to say so, for there are few sources of good news to be found and your visitor will be well aware of that.

Perhaps there could be a note that the morning sermons next month will be exploring issues of family life: 'What the Bible has to say about a good marriage', 'What the Bible has to say about living with teenagers', 'What the Bible has to say about old age'. If sermons are scheduled in this way, it is because God does have something to say and the gospel is relevant today. Do you not think it would be good to let your visitor know that serious issues of life are dealt with in your Church?

"IMPRESSIVE FACILITIES"

"THE SECOND ONE PRODUCES LAST WEEK'S SERMON"

James Jones, when Bishop of Hull, wrote, 'Many reordered church interiors do away with a pulpit, offering instead a flimsy portable contraption from which it would be difficult to give even the week's notices let alone a sermon.' Something of the same sentiment is expressed in the General Instruction of the Roman Missal (2,000) v.309: 'As a rule the ambo should be stationary, not simply a movable stand'. This is because the ambo is designed not only for reading and preaching but also for displaying the open Book of the Gospels or a copy of the Scriptures. It will be located in the sanctuary, the table of the Word alongside the table of the Eucharist, as a Roman Catholic might say. Other reordered churches may have an ambo taking the place of pulpit and lectern.

In spite of what the Bishop wrote, many preachers prefer to neglect the protection afforded by the pulpit and engage with their congregation at closer quarters.

If the pulpit is no longer used, why not tell your visitor that although teaching about Christian faith is given at most services, it feels right to some ministers to share the good news in a more conversational and personal way than is possible from the pulpit.

Lectern

Whether it is a copy of the Authorised Version, the Jerusalem Bible or the latest translation, most churches display a Bible; either on a lectern, an ambo, or on a table book stand. Could a recently used text be highlighted? It is doubtful that many would wish to use a marker pen for this, so why not think of a way in which the reading could be given prominence either by using the text on the page or by 'lifting it' in some way?

If there are two book ledges on the lectern, an illustrated or a children's Bible could also be displayed, with an invitation to take it down to show a small child. You may wish to say something of the authoritative nature of the Bible for Christian living. You could invite your visitor to take a free copy of a Gospel placed alongside the lectern or on the welcome table. Where there is no lectern, the Bible is often placed on a stand on the communion table to show word and sacrament together. It is unlikely that your visitor will understand this without your interpretation.

The font or baptistery

Baptism is always a time of great celebration; the coming together of biological families as well as faith families is a matter for rejoicing. There is, however, a special dimension to Christian baptism which has the potential of taking those gathered together into another realm. This could well be mentioned, as even visitors who know nothing of the Christian faith may have had some experience of a 'christening' and have remembered it as a very special time.

Many churches, as well as Baptist churches, now have baptismal pools but few of them will be open to inspection. On view or not, what about a photograph of someone being baptised (or a simulation as you may want to concentrate on worship during the actual baptism)? You may prefer a picture of the newly baptised, wet or dry, with a caption referring to their new life in Christ.

"I THOUGHT THERE WERE THREE BELIEVERS TODAY"

Where there is less water and a traditional font, the most frequent baptism will be of a child. The biblical image of being buried in baptism (Romans 6.4) does not fit well with the innocence of a small babe but the gospel shocks as well as saves and the theology should not be betrayed by too popular a comment. If the font is close to the main entrance, the reason for its location may be given. Some churches have baptismal rolls displayed on the walls but these will mean more to the congregation than to a visitor. To indicate that the church houses a living faith community there might be good reason to record the most recent baptism. A family photograph in a frame could work well with such words as:

Fight valiantly as a disciple of Christ
Against sin, the world and the devil,
And remain faithful to Christ to the end of your life.

It could have the name of the baptised and be on display for no longer than a month after which another photograph or a different aid to understanding would be appropriate. If special clothes or candles or oils are used in your church, could these sometimes be displayed with an outline of their faith story?

Altar

Traditionally – and church tradition goes back a long way – the most common site for the altar has been at the east end of the church building. Regrettably what should be the place of greatest unity has seen the greatest divisions. Even the word altar has been anathema to some and an unrecognised word to others. Communion table, holy table or just table are all describing the place where our Lord's words, 'Do this in remembrance of me', are obeyed. Whether you refer to the Mass, Breaking of Bread, Eucharist or Holy Communion, it is precious and central to the expression of communal worship.

Other churches have always had the communion table much closer to the people and nearly all reordering in recent years has resulted in the altar being moved nearer to the congregation.

In many churches, reordered or not, the altar will be within the sanctuary, into which visitors are seldom invited. Even so there is no need to keep secret the action which takes place there. As already mentioned, some congregations have the table laid throughout the week as a good way of explaining what happens. If that is not desirable, a tableau of similar vessels and linen could be arranged on a table inside the sanctuary close to where your visitor might walk. Any interpretation of this nature may well have to be moved aside for congregational worship but that will be no trouble for those who have already decided to adapt the church for the Monday to Saturday visitor.

There are many other items used in some churches in connection with the Eucharist, some of which remain to be seen such as the tabernacle and others of which are put away such as the censer. A decision will have to be made as to how detailed explanations are and that may depend on how central to the gospel each item is seen to be. Bear in mind that the work you are doing is for the benefit of the uninitiated rather than the faithful. An alternative approach would be to use a good photographic display with the emphasis on the spiritual impact of the vessels rather than their mechanical use.

Reserved sacrament – tabernacle

The existence of the reserved sacrament is always signified by a lamp. Any explanation will follow and be in sympathy with the previous interpretation of the Eucharist and may well be part of that interpretation.

Reordering is probably always contentious and compromises have resulted in some less than totally satisfactory arrangements. If there is a nave altar and the old, now probably called high, altar is still in place, the thought that has to be given to interpretation might lead to clearer thoughts on reordering! That slightly tongue-in-cheek comment does have a very positive aspect. It suggests that the thought put into the interpretation for visitors might lead to change in or renewal of existing furnishings or fabric. For instance, an arresting few words seen on a communion table over-cloth (or antependium, a word that designates all falls or hangings on the altar, pulpit and lectern), 'Turn to me and fulfil the only purpose for which you were created' is an adage which might work equally well on an external notice board.

> 'Turn to me and fulfil the only purpose for which you were created'

Stations of the Cross

Nowadays usually 14 in number – although that has varied – the Stations of the Cross depict the journey of Jesus to his crucifixion. They are paintings or reliefs or some other art form usually placed around the walls of the church. Some carry quotations from the Bible as well as a more standard wording describing each episode that is depicted. Both these and those Stations with no wording might benefit from an introduction. Your visitor might welcome a short description of the scenes and the way in which the stations are used in prayerful devotion.

Music and hymn books

The psalms are the Jewish hymn book and the style of song and the musical instruments are sometimes noted, along with the author. For example, Psalm 4 includes the direction, 'For the director of music: with stringed instruments'. In our day we can rejoice in a great variety of music. A reference could be placed close to the organ about 'making a joyful noise to the Lord' (Psalm 100). If your Church uses a band there may be some kit or stands around. If your music is provided by a CD player alone there will not be the same opportunity to tell your visitor about the music used in worship but you might well have discs playing for your visitor – an opportunity normally unavailable to organist, group or choir!

It may seem trivial to talk of hymn boards but the main services of the Church are unlikely to take place without the singing of hymns, songs and psalms. Those who are considering the gospel impact on a visitor may well leave hymn boards with last week's numbers to indicate that something was happening. That might be a fairly tenuous link but in the same way as the Bible text was highlighted so a gospel hymn could be displayed. In this context you might find that modern songs have very appropriate lines. Of course, if during worship, hymns are displayed by a digital projector, you might have to find a digital way to introduce them to your visitor!

"THE COMPETITION GOT A LITTLE OUT OF HAND"

Hassocks

Many congregations have put a lot of effort into making hassocks, enrolling both men and women in the process. Hassocks have often been counted integral enough to the life of a Church to have given rise to a special service of dedication. The designs portray all sorts of symbols and pictures and many reflect the area in which the church is situated and different organisations within the Church and community. They are usually colourful and add a measure of warmth to the building. Some carry words. Hopefully the cleaners at Westminster Abbey have a working knowledge of New Testament Greek as the hassocks in the quire need to be kept in the correct order to make sense. Your hassocks are probably not like that but what message might they proclaim to your visitors? You may be able to display them to convey a message relating to some aspect of the good news of God's love, rather than simply displaying parishioners' needlework skills.

Seasonal worship

Liturgical colours

Often churches have beautiful hangings which are changed according to the season. The colours used at different times tend to be the same although there are variations. Janet Strickler, an American artist, has suggested that the white used at Christmas is in contrast with the dark blue or purple that has preceded it in Advent, which was a colour of waiting: the colour of the sky just before dawn. With Christmas, the dawn has come; the Light of the World is here. This Light can shine into the darkest places, even the dark places within ourselves, and transform what it illuminates. Your interpretation could consist of a poster or other artwork: maybe even an old mandible or chalice veil in the colour of the season, along with an explanatory text.

With Christmas, the dawn has come; the Light of the World is here.

Advent

This book is focused on your visitor who may know nothing or very little about Christian faith and have no personal experience of a Lord and Saviour or a heavenly Father. Nevertheless, the primary purpose of the church building is to provide a space for worship by the people of God and the provision for visitors will need to be subordinated to that of the worshippers. The habit – by no means universal, even in traditional churches – of no flowers during Advent and Lent will certainly be a disappointment to some visitors. If the flowers on the welcome table are removed might it be appropriate to think of something beautiful to take their place?

Christmas

Christingle is the most well-attended service in many churches. Before the essential oils have evaporated from the orange a specimen christingle could be placed near the welcome table with a suitable explanation. In these days of digital imaging and almost instant quality pictures the christingle could be accompanied by a photograph showing something of the wonder and mystery of the celebration. You could provide a small bowl of sweets for the younger visitor with a request that the illustrative christingle is left complete.

A favourite display at Christmas both at home and in church is the crib. Rarely is it ordered with the pungent odours that would have been present in the stable of our Lord's birth but it does have a great appeal – which it might not if it were more authentic! The people and animals that are displayed are treasured and this applies whether they were handcrafted by members of the congregation or whether they have been paraded for more years than any-

"2 HEADS SINGED, A BURNT CHOIR ROBE,
WAX ON MY BEST SUIT, THE VICAR'S PHOTO!
FULL OF COCKTAIL STICKS LIKE A VOODOO
DOLL AND WE ONLY JUST PUT OUT THE
FIRE IN THE VESTRY"

"AND THEY LOOK LIKE ANGELS
IN THE CANDLELIGHT"

one can remember. This is surely an opportunity not to be missed in telling the gospel story. Alongside the crib could be placed an A5 sheet relating the reason for the incarnation and including a thanksgiving prayer with an invitation that the sheet be taken away and used.

Easter

The Easter garden is a well-loved feature in some churches. Adults may say it is for the children but it is as much for the older ones as is the crib. Of course the depiction is wildly out of proportion but nevertheless there is always some sort of cave with a stone rolled away and, in the background, three empty crosses. So meaningful you might think, yet an enquiry at the school or the supermarket would establish that the purpose of Good Friday is mainly related to hot cross buns – which have been on sale since the New Year – and Easter is about eggs and bunnies, usually of a chocolate variety, and spring flowers. The Easter garden needs an interpretation.

Good Friday is mainly related to hot cross buns.

Consider an invitation outside the church: 'Come and see our Easter garden'. Let the interpretation be biblically and theologically sound and easily understood. Here is another opportunity to have a few free leaflets on the meaning of Holy Week and Easter.

Stone and glass

This book relates to sacred buildings and the consecrated grounds around them, in particular the way in which the building might be used to communicate to your visitor the reason the building was constructed and for which it is still used. Yet even before a visitor receives the welcome that has been prepared, the building itself will have made an impact upon their senses. Following your welcome those feelings can be further developed by an invitation to stand and be still.

The building may be a Gothic colossus or a tiny old village church, a modern construction of glass and metal beams or a plain wood panelled meeting house. Each has its proportions and space, its shapes and its decoration and, at heart, its purpose as a place where people gather to worship.

Admittedly this aspect might be more difficult to appreciate in a worship centre that was built as a warehouse or erected a hundred years ago as a temporary construction with a corrugated iron roof, or in a dual-purpose building where the worship focus is curtained off during the week. But in the purpose-built church let there be a place to pause, to feel the space rather than the objects, to look up and to look around. Depending on visitor numbers you may be able to provide one or more places where there is an invitation to stand and be still, to enter into the past and present experience of many others who have come with their hopes and fears, their joys and their sorrows. A place where others have realised that there is not only a peace of silence but a more powerful and all-embracing peace, one that is personally offered by Jesus. A very short prayer could be displayed on a stand, 'God, give me your peace this day.'

"THEY HAD NO FAITH – IT WAS ALL DO IT YOURSELF"

"BUT DON'T YOU THINK IT'S BIT BIG FOR A CHURCH PLANT

Stained glass windows are often detailed and complex works of art containing a great deal of imagery and symbol telling a story directly related to the faith. Such windows need an interpretation. It is not easy, however, to read an explanatory text at eye level and then crane the neck to identify the

part of the window referred to. Some churches have a photograph of the window at eye level together with a description and interpretation. The millennium was marked by the commissioning of many wonderful windows. They are frequently simpler in design than older windows and what they illustrate is often easy to see. Yet although they might make an immediate impression on visitors they may still need faith interpretation.

Rood screen, the cross and the crucifix

For the first five centuries of the Christian Church the cross was not used as a symbol of the faith. The signs previously used were secret or cryptic: the fish, the anchor or the sacred monogram of X and P (the 'chi rho', standing for Christ). Now – and for many centuries – it would be most unusual to find a church of any denomination or style which does not contain at least one cross. It may be a plain wooden or metal cross or one with a figure which represents either a risen Christ (Christ in majesty) or a crucified Christ. The representation might be very small, say over a bookcase or very large, as on a rood screen which divides the nave from the chancel. Most of the figures above the screens were destroyed at the Reformation before which there would have been a crucifix often flanked by the Virgin Mary and the disciple John.

Within the faith interpretation of the building there is nothing more central than the cross, whether it represents the crucifixion or the resurrection. A simple explanation is not easy. Because the cross is widely used as a piece of jewellery by believer and non-believer alike it might be difficult to engage your visitor. Properly handled the very horror of crucifixion and the depth of humiliation and suffering our Lord underwent for you and for your visitor, should allow you to say something. It may even be appropriate to refer to the film *The Passion of the Christ* which aroused a great deal of interest, resulting in more than 2,500 enquiries being addressed to the Christian Enquiry Agency. Some of the viewers upon whom it made such an impact may well visit your church. Our understanding of the cross relates to the sin-bearing of Christ: whatever words of explanation are used, will you ensure that it is clear that his death was for us? Somewhere in the church why not have a cross to which is nailed a card:

> The cross was a method of torture and execution. Jesus died on a cross. 'Jesus gave himself for us to redeem us from all wickedness and to purify for himself a people that are his very own, eager to do what is good.' (Titus 2.14)

Consecration cross and the Bishop's chair

In churches where the office of bishop is recognised the church building will have been consecrated by a bishop. The evidence of this is a cross on the wall usually of paint, stone or metal. Originally there would have been 12 crosses but it may be that only one or two are now evident. A reference to these, or a bishop's chair (which, correctly, describes one particular chair in a cathedral but which may refer to a chair in a church which a visiting bishop might use) could be used to indicate that the congregation that lives in and works from your church sees itself as the local part of a universal body which the bishop represents.

> There may be only 25 who gather here week by week but we join with millions of others around the world who trust in the same God who cares for us all.

Please do touch

In some spiritualities, especially those quaintly called New Age, participants are encouraged to hold objects, for example crystals or rune stones. In church, however, it seems that nothing is close enough to touch. Perhaps it

"WE THOUGHT WE SHOULD GIVE THE CHILDREN A FEEL FOR CHURCH"

is not necessary for anything to be held during Christian worship but some Churches might want to introduce the Monday to Saturday congregation to an experience which allows a flower, say, or a small stone to be held or running water (recirculated) to be felt – a sacramental action carefully pointing, by its given description, to, say, the wonder of creation. Whatever is used could well relate to the local vicinity thereby acknowledging God both outside and inside the church building. Alternatively, visitors could be invited to hold a small plain wooden cross as the symbol of the Christian faith while their attention is drawn to its function as the means of a particularly brutal execution suffered by Jesus. If your church has a carving or some other piece of craftsmanship that moves people emotionally would you allow, or even invite, visitors to put their hand on it?

Banners and posters

In some ancient churches, as in old houses, there are still some tapestries or wall hangings, usually behind curtains or doors. Other churches have old and faded but beautifully crafted vestments. If you have any such treasure how might you use it in faith interpretation?

Beautiful banners evoke thoughts of power and movement, of creation and life.

With fewer gold threads and less silk than in the tapestries, there are many newer examples of beautiful banners and other fine needlework on altar cloths and pulpit and lectern falls. Some have clear and straightforward wording or liturgical references; others evoke thoughts of power and movement, of creation and life. There may be a seasonal motif or one that commemorates a special celebration. As with hassocks they are often created by a group working together within the congregation; sometimes they are bought from commercial manufacturers and religious houses. Such needlework or appliqué can be very powerful and in the main does not need interpretation. Place yourself in your visitors' shoes to decide what comment, if any, is necessary. Any interpretation could include the date and method of construction, as skilled craftsmanship is of general interest.

Much more temporary than worked banners are posters, sometimes of exactly the same design and size and others with simple representations and texts. These are often highly coloured, striking and attractive and, of course, a lot less expensive.

Heroes of the faith

By virtue of their great age, many churches appear to celebrate the dead rather than the living. Nevertheless the monuments, plaques and funerary tributes are often works of great craftsmanship: they are also cultural and historical records and sometimes testimonies to vibrant faith. It is possible that their existence is one reason people visit your church. Remember, however, that it is not only the dead whose achievements are worth celebrating. The church lives today. Use photographs and other material to promote the community work of your youth group, the local doctor who is on a short-term contract with a mission agency, the gap year student who is working on a mercy ship, or your previous minister – who you are still supporting – who has taken his family to an African country ravaged by HIV.

Other furnishings

An article in *The Times* in early 2005 claimed that there is an enormous interest in angels in contemporary non-Christian spirituality (along with 'yet more fads and frontier-busting in health, fitness and psychology'). *Equipping your Church in a Spiritual Age*, a workbook produced by the Group for Evangelisation, suggests that if your church has depictions or statues of angels you might develop them as a theme. You could disappoint your visitor by saying that angels, as described in the Bible, do not have wings but that would bring them down to earth unnecessarily: better to say that there are over 200 references to angels in the Bible where they are employed as God's messengers and agents!

An item that is still common in many churches is a copy of the Ten Commandments. At one time the law stated that they had to be displayed behind the holy table and they are sometimes still there, painted on the wall or on boards, often in rather

There is an enormous interest in angels in contemporary non-Christian spirituality.

poor condition. If they were on panels these may have been moved to another part of the church. The Ten Commandments were the foundation of much that was good in Western morality – to which a reference could be made.

Look around to see what carvings you have on an old parish chest or a screen or bench, coats of arms and hatchments, clocks and keys and ceiling decorations. They may not be too easy for the visitor to see in which case photographs might be appreciated. A number may have motifs which you can interpret but many items in old churches – and the 1984 report *English Churches and Visitors* referred to 155 different types of feature – largely reflect a secular interest to do with folklore, history and local culture. They included a witches' cauldron, a vamping horn and a fig tree with a curse on it. The last, at least, has a biblical precedent. Rejoice if these objects draw people into the building. Your visitors will also have the opportunity of learning something of the faith from your other work.

> *A witches' cauldron, a vamping horn and a fig tree with a curse on it.*

Audio and video guides

Many Churches have members with the skills to produce a simple audio guide for the building which can include a faith interpretation. Such guides will be especially appreciated by the blind and partially sighted. Listen to other sound guides and take advice as well. This need not be an expensive exercise: most churches will not need a large bank of equipment. Electronic devices are still getting cheaper and smaller but for your visitors the major factor will be ease of use: you may have to search around for something suitable.

Video is rather more ambitious, although a number of Churches are now employing it. Camcorders make filming easy, leaving the editing and dubbing to be expertly done. With some flair, the old furnishings and artefacts in the church could be made to come alive and the life of the Church can be recorded as it happens. Each film needs to be short and could be presented as a preliminary to a personal tour. References to the faith can easily be incorporated – let the faith shine forth from any members of the congregation who are featured. Keep the minister in the background!

A pilgrimage guide

The Christian Heritage of Northumbria project produced an excellent hand-book called *Sharing our Story* which included the following suggestion. It is similar to the labyrinth idea which is mentioned in Chapter 7:

> Visitors can be given a route to follow and encouraged to stop at particular spots for prayer or silence. This can be an excellent way of bringing the architecture to life. One Church that has tried this encourages visitors to begin by sitting in the porch and reading an extract from George Herbert's poem *The Church Porch*. They then move to sit by the church clock (whose works are visible) and reflect on a meditation about time. Under an ancient bell, dedicated to St Leonard, patron saint of prisoners, they read a poem by Irma Ratushinskaya and think about prisoners of conscience. At the altar they are drawn to the cross, which is worked with symbols of the four evangelists and hear the good news, 'He died that we might be forgiven'. The guide serves two purposes. It draws attention to the most interesting features of the church and, at the same time, enables your visitor to en-counter their significance. With imagination any Church can create one, or more, such 'spiritual guides'.

The handbook can be downloaded from: www.christian-heritage-northumbria. org.uk and then follow: project/press/dload/CHNhandbook.pdf.

Some questions to consider

- In what ways do we agree with the Church Heritage Forum quotation?
- How could we illustrate forgiveness or peace or wholeness or hope or love?
- Which items used in worship could we use to explain our faith?
- How will we select other items to illustrate God's love for us all?
- Is there any place or way in which our visitors can respond to God?
- Could we make enquires about the feasibility of an audio or video guide?

6

For Sale and for Free

The gospel is free

The good news of God's love is free. Much more to the point, the love of God himself is free: freely offered to any who will accept it. And because God loves us we can enter into a personal relationship with God the Father, God the Holy Spirit and God the Son, who is our Lord Jesus Christ. The book you are reading is theology. It is not academic theology but it is practical and down-to-earth theology. And 'down to earth' expresses the movement of God towards us, Jesus born for us, God with us.

Theology yes, but we do not need to use technical words such as 'incarnation' or words from an ancient language such as 'Emmanuel'. The message of God's love can be shared very simply. That is not to say there are no complexities or tensions in the gospel, nor does it mean that sharing the faith is reduced to one standard method. Your endeavour will be to share simply what is important to you – your own Christian faith.

The message of God's love can be shared very simply.

It is worth repeating that there should be no condescension towards your visitors but remember that perhaps many of your visitors will know little of God's love and even fewer will have entered into a relationship with him. So can they, freely and simply, be introduced to the idea of a loving God and even be offered the opportunity of taking something with them that might aid their journey to faith? Experience indicates that such grace will not increase the burden on the church finances, for it is well known – and could be described as a proven fact – that those who give away receive a greater income. There are often financial rewards for those who

"IT SHOULD HAVE READ, 'PLEASE TAKE A CARD' BUT THEY MISSED THE LAST LETTER"

work to improve what might be described as a good visitor experience!

The static information, the written or illustrated interpretations that you have provided, will remain in place for your next visitor but each individual visitor could be invited to take away an attractively presented Gospel or a prayer. 'Please take a leaflet' or 'The cards are for you' is all that is needed. At the Easter Garden a mini egg could be offered. Agencies such as the Christian Publicity Organisation and the Christian Enquiry Agency, and Lifewords (formerly Scripture Gift Mission) produce season-specific material that can be given away.

It has been suggested that if a free basic leaflet about the church is available then a better quality guide – even if it only costs £1 – will be left on the shelf. You may therefore decide that the attractive leaflet you offer, that gives a welcome in faith terms, will contain no information about the building. On the other hand, if you intend to share the faith you will certainly want the standard church guide to have a good faith content – whether it is a quality production or a freebie.

Earlier there was a recommendation that the church be visited to determine whether any of the good news of Jesus was being shared with your visitors. Another exercise would be to read the church guide and note how much of that is given over to faith sharing. Most commonly the faith is not mentioned at all or only obliquely. This raises a question as to what extent can faith and fabric be written about together? Too extensive a faith content could be counter-productive, causing the reader either annoyance or frustration: 'If I wanted to know about that I would have asked.' Would it be appropriate to reserve, say, just 10 per cent of the church guide for the faith, not necessarily as one block but in different places – such as one short section at the beginning and another at the end?

A Yorkshire Church has written this:

> This ancient church has been here at the top of the High St for centuries welcoming local people as well as folk from all over the world. It is a place where many have spent much time – looking, wondering, soaking up its atmosphere, worshipping, being still and quiet. It is the home of a large and vibrant Christian family. This is a place where many, each in their own way, are found by God. We hope you enjoy your visit to our church – and find something special here too.

Welcome leaflet

Hopefully those who come to Sunday services are welcomed and integrated; their objective is clear inasmuch as they come into the building to worship. When they first arrived, in the church or in the neighbourhood, they may have been given a welcome pack which told them about the Church family and about other organisations and facilities in the locality. That is excellent but such a pack will not be suitable to give to a visitor who is probably a tourist (for which the government definition is someone who has travelled more than ten miles). The welcome leaflet will be one of many things that you have to create specifically for your visitors. It may be offered on the welcome table or even before that – say, in a clearly marked holder outside the entrance door. In this case you may want to display a large word of welcome that all will see, with an invitation to take a leaflet. Of course, your welcome starts with the first signpost indicating the church is open, continues with a board by the porch, culminates with your welcome leaflet and is reinforced by the charm of your welcome table.

What will the leaflet say? As with everything else, the input and choice are yours, as there must be local ownership and a level of pleasure in the way the Church (the people) is taking the opportunity of sharing their faith with its visitors. The leaflet may be in the form of a declaration of the historic faith, it may refer to the way in which that faith has been exercised in your own Church, or your welcome leaflet may be a testimony of what the love of God means to your Church. Whatever the content, it should be quite short although it might point to other material that could be consulted. If you are majoring on interpreting the faith in other parts of the building the leaflet might invite attention to that and say very little itself. Decide whether it will offer the phone number of a member of your own Church who can be contacted although, bearing in mind that most visitors are not local, an invitation to contact the Christian Enquiry Agency or the Catholic Enquiry Office might be more suitable.

"ARE 59 PAGES ENOUGH?"

"PROBABLY. THE DETAIL IS IN A SEPARATE LEAFLET"

Giveaways

There are two categories of professionally produced written giveaways. First-ly there are publications which are free to you to use in your outreach; they are available on the condition that they are not sold but given away. A leader in this field is Lifewords. Secondly there are those companies that produce material for you to give away but for which you have to pay. Two of the best known are the Christian Publicity Organisation and the Christian Enquiry Agency. Of course, Lifewords need funds to carry on their work and they sensibly will tell you the value of the goods you order, leaving it to you to decide whether or not to support their work.

There are also notes in various formats and readership levels, designed to encourage people to read the Bible. Some publishers produce sample material; others will supply free out-of-date copies. You will probably already be in touch with one of these publishers: it might seem strange to encourage visitors to read the Bible if the congregation is not already so engaged. Could the same person look after the notes for both congregations, domestic and visiting? The Resources section contains information about such publications. Bookmarks, which have already been mentioned, and prayers to take away will be raised again in Chapter 7.

An area that might be new to some members of the congregation is the Christian press and organisations which are responsible for much mission work at home and abroad. Again the material for the Sunday and week-day congregations could be co-ordinated; there should be some well-displayed magazines in a rack with an invitation to read or, if preferred, take away. Many Christian magazines and newspapers are high-quality productions and would not look out of place in a newsagents' stand. They cover such subjects as development, ecology, politics, culture, media, music, and choir. Those members of the congregation who already subscribe could be encouraged to pass on their copies to the church stand and the Church itself may wish to subscribe to a Christian magazine not otherwise used within the Church.

Away from both proclamation and social work aspects of the gospel there is always the possibility of sheer grace which could reinforce the idea of the

Many Christian magazines and newspapers are high-quality productions and would not look out of place in a newsagents' stand.

gospel as a free gift. At least one Church invites its visitors to take with them a plant which, if it flourishes, may bring back happy memories of a good visit and, possibly, a reminder of the way in which life itself was freely offered.

St Nicholas', Blakeney, reported how a couple of holiday-makers appreciated their hospitality. Having felt overcharged and uncared for in holiday accommodation they called into the church. There was a dog bowl and an invitation to take him inside, where they were able to make a drink for themselves and have a biscuit without charge. When they had lit a candle and said a prayer they left with one of the gifts for visitors which members of the congregation place at the door. The notice alongside reads: 'We have a welcoming, hospitable God who gives us so much. We try to give others part of the experience we have enjoyed.'

A market place

One of the few episodes in the life of Jesus recorded in all four gospels is that concerning the temple traders. Jesus appears to have been livid with those who had a market in the Temple. This passage could have been at least partially responsible for the very idea of selling anything in a church being greeted with horror. Surely the sacred building should not be polluted by the profane: life inside and life outside the church building are legitimately distinct and separate. Is this the view our Lord would promote? We might conclude that the traders were interfering with the proper use of the house of prayer and maybe doing so in a dishonest way but this accusation would not be levelled against you! Another anathema was, or still is, the idea of eating and drinking in church, which is a little ironic as a meal is at the centre of the most sacred part of Christian worship. There is no intention here to introduce

"FUND RAISING IS ALWAYS EASY DURING AN INTERREGNUM"

arguments against such practices and beliefs but, hopefully, no offence would be given by asking whether the original reasons for these rules or habits are still valid.

"THEY'VE PUT IT BETWEEN THE MULLED WINE AND THE LOCAL CHEESECAKE"

The sales area

If you are happy to sell, you might think in three categories. The first is the sale of those items which are gospel-oriented: Bibles, testaments, books of prayer, devotional texts and Christian cards for various occasions. With your visitor in mind, stock some less expensive but well-presented booklets about the Christian faith (several are mentioned in the Resources section). The second is the sale of other items, such as mugs and tea towels with a picture of the church, and other useful items, often with a local label. A tour of a cathedral book shop will indicate the complete range. The third area is local produce which might include preserves, crafts and, less often, fresh produce. There is evidence that gospel items sell best when displayed with other goods, especially those produced locally. Grow lavender? Display it next to the book on a better marriage! Fair Trade shopping is becoming much more popular and if those goods are displayed there may even be a little impulse buying.

The book stall

Christian book shops have arrangements to support, financially and in other ways, the church book stall. Where there is a low turnover it may be difficult to keep books in good condition for what may be a considerable period of time, which indicates the need for very careful oversight. The potential purchaser likes to be able to look through a book before buying so ideally have a display copy to prevent the stock being spoiled. If members of the congregation have read the books themselves they may be able to lend their copy for display.

You may already have a book stall for your Sunday worshippers but it may not meet the needs of your Monday to Saturday congregation. There are inexpensive titles that deal with the kind of questions that may be in the minds of your visitors. Can rational people believe in God? How do you find a faith to live by? How to cope with bereavement, serious illness, debt, broken relationships, depression? Some books do not attempt to answer such questions but provide prayers for people to use.

There are many Christian books for children dealing with both life and death. Some titles for both adults and children can be found in the Resources section.

The money

You have agreed to take a large risk by having your church open to visitors and unhosted Churches will have to take a further risk in respect of their wares and the payment for items that are bought. The best security for money that has been received might well be frequent removal rather than attempting to replicate the safety of a local bank vault. A person local to the church may be prepared to empty the box twice a day. When that is not enough, the time has probably come for full-time hosting.

Some questions to consider

- Is there an adequate faith content in our church guide?
- How much can we budget for items that we give to our visitors?
- Can we ask a retailer for help in presenting our sales area?
- What assistance will the local (or not so local) Christian book shop give us?
- Could we sell local produce or crafts without undermining local shops?
- What will we have, free and for sale, that will appeal to children?

7

The House of Prayer

Prayer – powerhouse of mission

One of the distinctive things about a vibrant Christian community is its commitment to prayer. There appears to be an inextricable link between prayer and all mission work. As you put into place some of the approaches mentioned in this book you are engaged in mission work. As you pray you will be expecting your visitors to find a sustaining faith in a loving God although in all likelihood what happens in your church will be only a part of an ongoing process.

Do visitors to a National Trust castle, on reading the explanatory boards immediately become archaeologists? Are those gazing at the railroad giants in York Railway Museum instantly transformed into a new generation of trainspotters? You know it is not quite like that but how wonderful if everything you are providing for or even saying to your visitors reflects your own enthusiasm and experience. As you read this book, ask God how you can engage with your visitors. Ask him how you can share your love and how you can invite visitors to seek after the living God – or be found by him. If you have welcomers it would be good if, as part of their brief, they were also engaged in prayer for your visitors.

Providing a prayer area

Faith sharing in our cathedrals is as little practised as in most other churches but one aspect that is common in these buildings is an invitation to pray. A space is set aside, with other visitors being asked to pass by silently. But

prayer is not the reason most people have entered the building and so the positioning of the prayer area needs to be well considered. The cathedral at Tours in France has half the nave allocated for prayer; this may demonstrate an impressive faith on the part of the authorities but may not give those praying the peace they desire. In your planning remember that an invitation to pray in, say, the Lady Chapel may mean nothing to the unchurched or even to some Christians from Nonconformist backgrounds. Some further indication of the allotted area would be helpful.

The invitation to pray rarely indicates to whom prayer is made; it is considered implicit, thought to be obvious. Knowing, however, how many gods there are within the enormous number of spiritualities that are followed in our day, you may wish to draw attention to our faith in God; Father, Son and Holy Spirit. It would be absurd to erect a large notice reading, 'Only prayer to the triune God is allowed' but there are gentler ways of encouraging people to know that Christians believe not simply in prayer itself but in the One to whom the prayer is made.

An easy way to encourage your visitor in that direction is to provide an invitation to pray and to offer some prayers that could be used. The invitation to pray at Bradford Cathedral is in these words:

> In the Name of Jesus Christ, we welcome you to our church.
> Here in the quiet you may speak to God.
> Here you may give thanks:
> Here you may cast your burdens upon Him:
> Here you may seek strength for the present and courage for the future,
> Then go on your way rejoicing:
> And may God bless you
> And grant you his peace evermore.

Many churches do have places designated for private prayer. In a large building the area set aside need not be close to the most popular walkway. A small single-span building may have to choose a corner that is not needed for Sunday worship. If that is not convenient the prayer area may have to be set up for the week and reordered for Sunday. It would be good if there was somewhere to kneel, even if few visitors would adopt that posture. Many would prefer a comfortable seat; an upholstered lounge chair would be better still. While mentioning comfort, is it possible that the silence in a church is disturbing? On Sunday the organ thunders, on Monday it is all 'Shhhh!' If there is no music in the church as a whole, would it be possible to have it in the prayer area? Not easy, but worth thinking about – unless you think it would then feel like a funeral chapel.

Aids to prayer

Try to place some aids close to each chair so they can be accessed easily. You could offer 'official' prayer books if they can lay open on a shelf or rail; individual prayers with general or specific topics; encapsulated cards; books made of plastic sleeves with pictures one side and prayers opposite. There could be a book that opens flat titled, 'Pray with the Day', holding pictures of morning, noon and night or the four seasons with just a few words on each page. This may help those not used to praying to be able to look, think, and perhaps pray and give thanks. A verse of scripture well displayed, icons, pictures and other physical objects as well as flowers may be helpful to some. You will probably have some form of cross or crucifix and maybe a candle.

Prayer requests

There are various ways in which prayer requests can be handled. Let your visitors know that their requests will be taken to a service, or a meeting for prayer, on a specified day or within a given time. Prayers can be left pinned to a board, hung on a tree, fastened to a net, placed next to a cross or left in a box so they cannot be read by everyone. Try to make your system simple and easy to use. If the approach to the prayer area is at all dark it would be more comfortable if it were lit in some way. Provide paper, as well as a couple of pens so that when one is inadvertently pocketed there is still one available. The paper need not be blank. It could indicate what happens to a prayer request; it could also have a pre-printed verse from a Psalm or a promise from a Gospel. If there is an invitation to pin the request on a prayer tree, paper could be in the shape of a leaf.

If there are people willing to support your visitors you will be able to offer a name and phone number that can be contacted in the same way as you may have done on the welcome leaflet. The times of services and an invitation to attend could be displayed in the prayer area as well as in other suitable places. A notice about healing services might also be welcomed by people who stop to pray.

Prayer stations

Labyrinths and Prayer Stations, a Grove booklet by Ian Tarrant and Sally Dakin, suggests, as an aid to prayer, the creation of temporary stations placed within the church and worked around a parable or biblical episode. Although the idea can readily be seen as an excellent spiritual exercise for members of the congregation the authors actually say of potential visitors: 'people are encouraged to come in . . . to make their journey . . . Could this be a form of evangelism?'

The answer is in the affirmative. This idea is not as direct as most of the other suggestions you have considered so far but it will appeal to some.

In cathedrals and larger churches there may be prayer broadcast around the building. Westminster Abbey has prayer at 10 am, 11 am, noon and then twice in the afternoon. Visitors are invited to stand still, they are welcomed, a thought is given and that is followed by a prayer. An invitation is then given to join in the Abbey worship and finally a 'blessing' is pronounced. All this, by order of the Dean, should be done within 60 seconds. Just imagine what could be done in two whole minutes! The impact on the visitor may not be known but even in such a national shrine those who enter are reminded that the primary purpose of the building is Christian worship.

Candles

Candles are very popular. They need to be a little distance from the prayer area. Whatever fire precautions are deemed necessary should be in place. Many churches display a card, such as the following, describing why a candle is often used in prayer.

To find the words for a prayer is difficult,
We do not know what to say.
Our hearts are too full for words,
Our anxieties paralyse.
The Holy Spirit acts for us,
Himself speaking the words to God.
Light a candle,
Let the Holy Spirit work,
Let him lead you in prayer.

Remembering the way in which Jesus welcomed those who had no learning, no understanding and no maturity – his reference to little children may embrace all of these – you may even feel free enough to print a bold notice:

Don't know what to say? Don't know how to pray? Light a candle!

If you have a candle card for visitors to take, a prayer that may be known could forge some sense of identity:

O Holy Spirit
Make me a channel of your peace.
Where there's despair in life let me bring hope,
Where there is darkness let me bring light,
And where there's sadness, joy.
O grant that I may never seek
So much to be consoled as to console,
To be understood, as to understand,
To be loved, as to love with all my heart.

Incense

Sometimes incense has been used to disguise otherwise unwelcome church smells! For its use there needs to be a person in attendance. As an alternative try lighting an aromatic candle. The fragrance may help to make the place of prayer different and, in a way, special.

Some questions to consider

- What is our present provision for visitor prayer? Can we improve (or create) it?

- What aids to prayer do we provide? Should we have pictures, icons or flowers?

- What provision do we make for prayer requests, to receive them and to pray them?

- Do we pray for our visitors apart from their requests? When might we?

- Candles are better in a separate area. Can we implement sensible safety measures?

- Is our church at all musty? How can we either correct it or introduce a fragrance?

8

Younger Visitors

What will they remember?

Of all our visitors, children are the least likely to come of their own volition. They will come with their family or as part of a school group or youth organisation. The research on which *Rural Visitors* (Acora 2001) was based revealed that 5 per cent of visitors were under 12 years of age and 11 per cent between 12 and 19. Most of the latter group would be offended to be called children and there will be vastly differing levels of interest and understanding. The research showed that this whole group was more interested in the visitors' book, the flowers, the music, the smell of incense, the candles, and the open Bible, than any other age section. It follows that the more the senses are stimulated the better. Especially among the young there will be many caught up by mystery and space and by sight, sound and colour; such things could be the beginning of their understanding of what God has done for them. Research must have its groupings, of course, but from a practical point of view once the visitor is, say, over 15 years of age, it is difficult to see that any special provision can be made.

School parties will come for one of two purposes: to worship or to fulfil part of the curriculum. In both cases the school will bring prepared material. If the purpose is to worship there is likely to be an established relationship between school and congregation. If the visit is educational, permission will have been obtained and so it would be possible to give them a personal welcome. The school curriculum notes: 'Visits provide opportunities for reflections on beliefs and values, and allow children to respond with awe and wonder to the atmosphere or to something that is beautiful or special.' There is still a statutory obligation to ensure that an agreed syllabus reflects that the religious traditions in Great Britain are in the main Christian.

There is thus a great challenge: how should the church be presented to younger visitors during the week? The Scripture Union book, *Top Tips on Reaching Unchurched Children* opens with a reference to Liam, aged 7, who declares he knows nothing about God other than he made the world, information gleaned from his dad. A few pages later there is a reference to the newspapers' reports that David Beckham wanted to have his son Brooklyn christened although he didn't know into which religion. In spite of being repetitive it is worth saying again that many visitors have little or no knowledge of Christianity. Visiting children have had even less chance to learn than their parents.

You may wish to tell children that the font is used for baptism, signifying entry into the Christian faith, but could you make it live and have a greater impact? The same question can be asked at each point in the church where some specific activity takes place. Visiting schoolchildren are more likely to be local than most other visitors, in which case they are children with whom you could possibly re-establish contact. It would be good to ensure that such explanatory material that has been devised to be taken away includes an invitation to a Church activity. You have happily agreed to a visit and, by working with the school, you could enhance it. That afternoon the normal visitor welcome notice could be changed to a specific welcome to that particular school. You will have ensured that the lights are on and perhaps even the heating! Could you afford to give each child a bookmark with an assurance of God's love for them? Consider well the impression that will remain with the children: will they want to return?

One thing is easier with children than with adults and that is obtaining a response to the visit, on which can be built ideas for engaging children in the future. The following pieces were written as part of a primary school exercise by children attending a school with close links to the Church. They may suggest to you how to make the children's visits more interesting or productive and how they might learn at an early age of the nature of Christian faith. There were 12 pieces contributed to a magazine of which 9 used the word

'feel' and yet, from their writing, it is clear that much more than the building, its space and light and colour, has influenced them. They have clearly been given other information about Christian beliefs and practices, although it is a little surprising to read about the location of the marriage ceremony!

> When I go inside a church I feel happy because it reminds me of Jesus. We sing lots of songs about Jesus and God. You see a stained glass window. You sometimes get a hot cross bun. People get married and christened in a font. The thing that you sit on is called a pew. Some people have parties. There is a candle on the altar because Jesus is the light of the world.
>
> Sam, aged 7

> When I go to church I feel the words of God. They say to me 'thank you for coming to my holy place.' When I am in church I pray to God and respect him. I pray to God about things that make me sad and I ask him to sort things out. When I am praying in the church the blue and green stained glass window soothes me. Outside the church feels soothing and soft and I can still hear the words of God. The church is a place to pray and respect God. That's why I like the church so much. God will always be with us.
>
> Helena, aged 8

Hundreds of Churches host school visits: here are notes from just two.

Castle Hill Baptist Church, Warwick

One of the most encouraging groups of visitors that any church building can welcome are schoolchildren. We have steadily built excellent relationships with some of the local schools, both primary and secondary, inviting them, for instance, to come and compare our building with those from different faiths or other Christian traditions. This has proved to be a remarkably easy way to get people who wouldn't normally have Christian contact to step across the doorway and to ask questions.

In turn we are presented with a wonderful opportunity not just to explain what we do, but also why we do it this way. A huge amount of theology can be communicated in an interesting way that challenges young people and sometimes their teachers, to think about the reason why people have gathered in this place for hundreds of years.

Coventry Cathedral

Most children visiting here have very positive comments about their visit. We especially like remarks such as, 'I thought it was going to be really boring but it was really good'.

We find the smells of a building make almost more impact than the sight and sound! So easy to get this one wrong: musty, dusty, old and uncared for, as opposed to rich, warm, scented, incense, candles, flowers. Food and gifts and generosity are also key ways of making church visits more rewarding and not just for children!

If we keep the door open and have love and a welcome in our hearts that is what they will remember.

From pushchairs to pre-teens and beyond

Trailing behind adults is boring. Not being able to see things because they are placed at adult height is discouraging. Not understanding because the presentation is aimed at an older audience is frustrating.

You may already have decided to leave the children's corner intact. There may be soft toys and, for the older ones, Bible story books. A notice that says, 'Please play with our toys and books' may be unintelligible to the younger children but they will soon get the idea!

For older children a good idea is a colourful pack which they can be invited to use and take away. You may wish to draw attention to it at adult height and ask for a modest payment, which most parents would gladly contribute in return for a happy child. And the child would be happier still if a binding ribbon for the pack also held a lollipop.

A limited number of 'I spy' questions might be appropriate; some of them giving pictures of objects to be found. List the questions in the same order as the objects thus attempting to prevent the excited child from terrorising the place while searching for successive answers.

The child would be happier still if a binding ribbon for the pack also held a lollipop.

Encourage the children to touch things – an activity often discouraged elsewhere – in order to 'join' with people of long ago who also visited the church. Have a picture Bible and invite the children to turn to a numbered page to find a word to complete a verse on their paper. Give them a different coloured piece of paper with a simple prayer on it and invite them to take it to a place set aside for them to pray. Suggest that they say a prayer of their own, perhaps writing it on the sheet. Remember the seasons of the year and of the Church and include something – which could be one of dozens of items professionally produced by a Christian publishing house – that refers to, say, Christmas or Easter if those times are near. Overall, try not to make it like a school exercise: do enough to keep their interest but provide only enough for the average visiting period.Give them a chance to see 'funny' things their parents might miss. These could be included in a journey home activity in which they could quiz their parents' observation. Your paper could conclude 'Please come to see us again.' A jar of biros and other writing tools would be helpful.

Engaging their attention

Children of all ages have something in common: they like to be treated as real people, important in their own right. They often have an enormous attention span for Playstation and other addictive pastimes but rather less for an experience where they are not propelled along the storyline. Living museums capture attention by allowing children to enter another time zone with all its peculiar sights, sounds and smells. You might be horrified at the idea of allowing children to dress up or encouraging them to enact being burned at the stake with the use of the votive candles but the question is, what can be done to enhance their experience? And – this is the significant part – how will we let the children know that they are as important to God as anyone else? Hopefully in nurturing our own Church children we have not made God smaller in order to fit them: neither must we for our young visitors.

Why not invite the children to stand next to a cross scratched in the wall by a crusader's sword at the end of his prayer vigil? Allow their imagination to picture the scene, with the knight kneeling before the altar – no communion rail in those days. Or could they review the life of someone who lived in the same town or village by counting the steps from the font at baptism to the chancel steps at marriage and then to the tombstone in the churchyard? To see records of the events in the old registers would make it extra special. The Christian implications of the rites of passage should be an integral part of the story.

The young visitor may have an even greater sense of a special and sacred space than the adults they come with, although if they say anything it may only be 'wow' or 'cool' – which may be climatically accurate – or 'wicked' – which, hopefully, is far from the truth. In respect of the language of the young this text is out of date as it is written as their usage changes quicker than the weather. Let us simply recognise the privilege of telling children in a straightforward way that God loves them and wishes to have an ongoing relationship with them.

Recognise the privilege of telling children in a straightforward way that God loves them.

What is it for – with spin

Helmsley Parish Church has a special guide for children which responds to their wish to be involved. There are, for instance, a number of good and mature suggestions for prayer to accompany the lighting of a candle. When it comes to describing implements which adorn the church wall the guide encourages the youngsters to continue in prayer, in God conversation, in an interesting way:

The pikes on the wall at the side of the font were used in medieval times by constables to keep order in the town and stop people fighting and squabbling. The flag is that of a special band of soldiers who were connected with Helmsley and fought in the last war to guard our country's freedom. Seeing these things can move us to say a big thank you to God for all those who protect us so that we can live in safety.

Some questions to consider

- In what ways could our younger visitors know that they matter to us?

- Could we work with a local school on a faith and fabric project for a guide book?

- Can we leave things out for younger children to use while their parents look around?

- 'Younger' covers a range of intellect and size. Can we grade material in Key Stages?

- How could we keep in touch with local children who visit?

- How do we encourage children to pray and to respond to God?

9

Church and Community

In Chapter 1 we asked who our visitors are and why they come and it was claimed that in the main people come from a distance and for no specific purpose or, at least, for no purpose that had been decided well in advance.

There are, however, several other groups of visitors who come intentionally and not from a distance.

Local community

Members of the local community, especially in rural areas, often enjoy a sort of long-term semi-ownership of the church which might not extend to other than rare attendance at public worship. They visit because it is their church and sometimes perhaps with the specific intention to pray or to absorb the peace. They will also visit if the church is a source of information they require. You may wish to offer not just the material prepared for your visitors but immediate and timely social support. Stress, breakdown and addictions are problems of our age: display details of how to contact Samaritans and Relate and other such organisations. Further assistance could be given on a card with telephone numbers of members of the congregation who are equipped to offer help in contacting counsellors and carers. The card could also outline any local pastoral care that is available and it could offer prayer – even to the existence of a prayer surgery at the local medical centre, as advertised by a church in Patterdale.

Why not arrange for your church to be a tourist or community information point?

Information about local events

In town centres and holiday areas it is often possible to find a Tourist Information Centre but elsewhere it is far more difficult to obtain comprehensive information about local events and activities.

As a public building why not arrange for your church to be a tourist or community information point? You could house the board or leaflet holders in the porch rather than inside the church. Alongside local events and attractions think of advertising your own bereavement support group, helping-hand team and mothers' and toddlers' club.

In some rural areas without a shop, the daily newspapers are delivered to the church porch from which subscribers collect them.

Community use of the building

In recent years there has been a growing awareness that the church buildings we have inherited, which are often a great burden to the congregation, should be made available for others. In former days the church building was the community hall and sometimes the court, the market place and the theatre; even the fire station or the armoury. The part of the church towards the east end was used for sacred purposes and the other end for the profane. Today with more joined-up thinking, more use is being made of the space the church building affords. Churches are taking the initiative and returning the building to community use. As *Open All Hours: A Way Forward for Church Buildings in the 21st Century* (Acora) says:

> There are a variety of reasons for opening up churches for community use. An open church demonstrates the welcome of God to all people. A locked church turns people away from God.

"WHY IS THERE A TOP SHELF?"

"JUST TO SHOW THERE'S NOTHING ON IT"

In reordering some churches have simply divided the space by reserving the chancel, choir and sanctuary areas for worship while releasing the nave for other uses. Others have been reordered so that the whole area is available for varied use, although nothing must be allowed to conflict with the primary use of the building as a centre for worship. Reordering with more building work has produced a series of rooms which provide accommodation for a variety of purposes. What all these arrangements have in common is that local people who may not normally worship will be visiting the church. Some may not even think of it as a church; others might even conclude that the Church is dead and no longer needs its building. It would indeed be sad if the reason for reordering or redeveloping was simply to balance the budget, ignoring the opportunities offered to tell visitors about the love of God. Hopefully the mission aspect would be considered before any building scheme is put in place. As a result there might even be a perceived advantage in providing an entrance hall, well apportioned and furnished, through which people will not just rush but will linger, to see and to listen – or just to feel at peace.

Those from local communities who enter their neighbourhood church will always be interested in a rogues' gallery – the office holders and workers within the Church. Would you consider having a 'mug of the month' in order to highlight one particular person, together with their testimony to God's work in their life?

Community service

There is a great deal of wonderful community service offered by Churches across the land. It would take a very large book even to catalogue it. Much, indeed most, of the work is done from premises other than the church building where weekly worship takes place. Nevertheless there is an increasing community use of the church building itself.

People may be initially suspicious of some of the regular activities just because they are held in a church. These might include mothers' and toddlers' clubs, crèche, play groups, lunch clubs, space for men, tea and chat, bereavement groups and many more such as coffee shops and cafés, internet halls, book shops, drop-in centres, farmers' markets, post offices, grocers, nearly new clothes and even automatic cash dispensers.

Some work may seem to be no more than an adjunct to statutory services although it is not to be derided for that. Other activities have a definite Christian ethos. In either cases paid staff or volunteers are often clearly motivated by the love of God. These activities and necessary alterations to buildings to enable them to take place, have often been funded by government or local charities.

Funding schemes are always changing and may be available for a short period only. Public schemes will be published on the World Wide Web as well as in more traditional ways. There are many websites for local charities as well and a visit to the local library might be worthwhile. Promotion of Christian faith is not an objective for which public funds are available even though life-styles opposed to the faith are often heavily supported from central funds. Nevertheless, applications for activities that support the community and promote cultural heritage (and Christianity is very much part of that) do fall within many funding guidelines. In addition, mechanisms for delivery – to use bid document terms – can show the Church as a catalyst and the Church can figure as the prime resource for delivery of any specified aim. Funding is often crucial when a local Church needs to engage in a building programme but is well outside the scope of this book. A word with someone in a central Church office would be a place to start but it is not a matter of one phone call: access to funding is often a long and arduous road needing persistence and dedication.

Even where community activities take place in an adjacent church building rather than the worship centre itself, there may be mobile displays that could be moved from the church, together with book trolleys and other items. As an alternative you may be able to encourage people to enter the church or even have the access or exit through the church building.

Before moving to short descriptions of specific community activities, there follows a quotation that might make sense to you. It comes from *Rural Mission* (Acora 2002) a workbook which addressed issues in the countryside but which has a more universal application.

> As the church building is used in ways that are recognisably useful for the community new connections will be made ...

St Paul's, Walsall have a project within the church building called 'The Crossing'. In one of their leaflets they give the reason for community use of the church building; a reason that could be universally true and which led to the selection of the name of their project: 'The Crossing refers to the meeting point of church and community, as well as to the crossing over from death to new life in Jesus, which is at the heart of the Christian faith.'

To move from suggestion to experience, here are a few comments from those who have decided to use their buildings as a community resource, starting with St Paul's, the size and scope of which is beyond the imagination of most!

St Paul's, Walsall

Three floors now occupy the shell of the old church. There is a day chapel on the ground floor with the main worship area on the second. Visually everything is joined by the light well. There are seven retail units on the ground floor, with the Day Chapel being open throughout the week for prayer and reflection. The first floor includes a coffee shop seating 70, together with offices for the Church and others. The second floor has the main worship centre and that and ancillary rooms are used for a wide variety of functions. There is a priest on duty at all times and staff are willing to talk to and befriend callers and customers.

Castle Hill Baptist Church, Warwick

We have found it very beneficial to be blessed with a coffee shop as part of our church building complex. This former pub is now integral to the architectural layout of our new building, and enables the volunteers to show visitors around the church itself. This has led to a large number of quite detailed conversations about the building, which in turn leads to discussion about what is important in a church building and why.

The café also provides a non-threatening way to attract people into an environment where they meet Christians and are offered a listening ear and a potential for prayer. Many people take advantage of our strategically placed prayer book where we offer to remember those who are entered, during our regular Church prayer meetings.

Christchurch (Methodist/URC) Ilkley

We concentrate on maintaining an environment of friendly fellowship in our coffee centre which has roughly 2,000 customers a week. There are free booklets and there is a Christian book stall and posters and cards invite customers to our services. On three days a week a member of the

pastoral team is present to offer a listening ear. Some young people with learning difficulties take part in our work experience schemes. There is a shoppers' service on Fridays. The worship area is open every day.

St Margaret's, Kings Lynn

Our church café closes at the beginning of Lent and reopens in May. The autumn café has a distinct clientele: not summer visitors but local shoppers, market traders and congregation members who are regulars and enjoy the sociable atmosphere as much as the food. We regard this as vital community outreach to encourage local people to cross the threshold. Once a month a Russian Orthodox group uses the side chapel beyond the café for their liturgy; this is liked by customers, who often sit longer over their coffee to listen to their music.

Camborne Methodist Church

We have now crossed the VAT threshold for our café and have set up a limited company for the Wesley Centre at the rear of the worship area.

Grant funding has been received for a community worker who we hope will be able to assist in faith communication.

Bunyan Meeting Free Church

The coffee shop is in the foyer of the church and is open five days a week for four hours. There are Christian posters and leaflets covering the Church programme. Alongside others we employ some staff with learning difficulties. There is always someone available to talk or pray with visitors.

West Bradford Methodist Church

The village post office was in a family home and when they retired it was not possible for the PO to continue to use that building.

We had a room at the front of our church, which had really been an old junk store for many years. A considerable amount of work on the premises was necessary to raise it to PO standards, who referred to it as a Dedicated Post Office, which for them meant it had the sole use of one particular room, but for us could mean something more in line with our faith!

The arrangement works very effectively for the Methodist Church. It means that people come on the premises who would not normally enter the church. And it means that we are providing a community facility which is needed within the village.

St Chad's Centre, Wolverhampton

We run Tele Resources, a project designed to help young people from the black and minority ethnic communities who have been unemployed to obtain training, experience and qualifications in tele sales and marketing. We placed 55 young people into full-time work in the first 12 months of the project.

We make sure that events are publicised to all callers to the church projects, with posters and hand bills. The Christian faith is presented through our displays, and by linking projects to special services through-

out the year. We sometimes provide transport for the elderly to be able to attend these services. We have also trained members of the congregation to be community chaplains, and to be there to listen and respond.

St Nicholas' Church, Great Yarmouth

We are in the heart of Great Yarmouth and a popular tourist attraction. We try to provide a place of peace and welcome to holiday-makers and townspeople alike. We have a clothes store that is open in the church for anyone needing not only clothes but bedding, small furniture, books, toys and someone to talk to. The coffee shop provides a place for people coming to the store to sit, talk or just come in out of the rain. As more people realise that the church is open we find that we need to provide much more than coffee and gifts. The chance to find someone to talk to, who will listen but not judge, is being taken up with greater frequency.

Sometimes we experience something quite remarkable. One of our volunteers had her purse stolen. Many months later a young woman came in, described the volunteer and asked if she was in the church. The reason for her visit was to return the money, which she had stolen to feed a drug habit. The young woman was now free of drugs and her visit to the church had been the start of her freedom.

Central Methodist Church, Burnley

The 'Basement' project caters for youngsters between 11 and 18. Meeting 2 or 3 times a week it is building bridges between us and the ethnic communities. The café is on the ground floor. We display literature that can be taken away. There is a weekday service that a few customers join.

Stowlawn Anglican Methodist LEP Church

We have set up the Faith Regeneration Unit, supporting Churches from every denomination, and other faith groups in building their capacity to develop their churches, by raising funds for buildings, staff and projects.

St Leonard's, Bilston

In St Leonard's we run the Senior Citizen Link Line, as well as the Melting Pot Café and recreational classes. The first project is a proactive telephone support service for older people, most of whom are vulnerable, isolated and lonely. We currently phone 1,500 people every week. We have used vestries and Sunday school rooms, converted for different uses on Sundays and during the week! We now employ ten full-time staff on this project, as well as numerous volunteers.

Southport Salvation Army Citadel

From our church building we run the following: Young at Heart Club (ages 50 plus), 'Kidz Klub' (7–12 year-olds), Parents and Toddlers once a week and Ladies' Fellowship weekly. In the church we have a booklet stand, with specially selected items and posters announcing events and courses which have evangelical potential. Other printed material includes our own

War Cry, Kids Alive, weekly newsletter and prayer list together with CPO posters, which are regularly changed to communicate major Christian themes.

We have a specially prepared prayer room which is open to all and we serve Fair Trade goods and display posters highlighting them. We also have staff who love God and who are ready to listen to our customers and to explain their faith.

Leeds Methodist Mission

We run Person-to-Person, a listening service, as a drop-in from Monday to Friday as well as the café. Leaflets about Christian faith, forthcoming services and other events are always around.

St Ives Free Church, Cambridge

Just Sharing is the name of our Fair Trade shop, which has a turnover of more than £90,000 per annum. There is a very good, well-constructed and lit display board in the entrance hall that is seen by everyone who enters the building. The Church spent a lot of money on this and it is used only for displays about the Christian faith.

St Stephen's, Norwich

Visitors from the continent were shocked at the talking, laughing, eating and drinking in church at our *Refreshment Centre*. They were soon joining in all these things and a discussion followed about Jesus and how he met the physical needs of the crowds before teaching them about God and the kingdom. Organists are allowed to play and singers are encouraged to test the acoustics.

Being a city-centre church, there have been regular visits by the homeless and those in hostels. Sometimes they wear their caps, and maybe bring in a dog: we reckon to cater for the whole person – and their four-footed friends.

St Peter's, Hereford

We have a permanently running slide show on the theme, 'What do these stones mean?' as a guide to the Christian faith. On Wednesdays we offer a lunchtime discussion over coffee on any topic that any visitor wishes to raise. On Thursday lunchtime the topic is 'How my faith affects my work' again with coffee and sometimes sandwiches and on Friday lunchtime, there is a 30-minute opportunity to join in prayer or to receive prayer with the laying on of hands.

Bill, a man in his sixties, had been dropping in from time to time. A few months ago one of our stewards said, 'Great seeing you on Wednesdays – but why not come on a Sunday?' Bill has made that step, and tells all his friends that Sunday is now the best day of his week. And two weeks ago, he went to the local book shop, and bought himself a Bible, which he uses on Saturdays to read through what we are going to be studying in church the next day.

St Mary of Bethany, Woking

We had an excellent Election Day (5 May 2005). We had the church open from 6 am to 10.30 pm, and served tea, coffee and cakes all day. At least two Church members were on duty all the time. We had three displays in the entrance hall, including notices of our work in the community, two Ascension Day communion services, a youth band practice and Steve and Nancy singing for a period. We had a PowerPoint on a loop throughout the day showing many different aspects of church with background music. Many people stopped to talk. As a direct consequence, three people joined an Alpha course and became regular church attenders, two came to an older person's group and one asked the minister to visit.

Inviting others to use the church

St Ives Free Church, Cambridge, mentions many activities that take place which are not necessarily run by Church members. They have two mental health groups, Cruse Bereavement Care, Arthritis Care, Civic Society, art groups, a photographic society, a volunteer bureau, and RSPB. Other Churches host local clubs such as gardeners, the local history society and the debating society. Less regular events such as musical concerts, art festivals and exhibitions and flower festivals often work extremely well in a church. Canon Keith Orford writes that in the East Midlands churches are the main venues for the performing arts and this could be the case in other regions as well.

The lack of toilet facilities in many church buildings has been mentioned before. Another difficulty for some Churches is the absence of facilities to prepare and provide refreshments. The legislation in this area needs to be followed yet it is becoming so detailed that even small commercial catering firms are finding life extremely difficult. In spite of these problems the use of the church for secular activities is a revenue raiser and appealing in its own right. Let us continue to be aware of the opportunity we are given when people who might not normally cross the threshold are keen to enter.

Depending on the occasion and the arrangements made with event organisers, it could be that the more prominent items of your visitor welcome and the faith interpretation have to be put away when some outside groups use the building. In this case you could consider offering guests, on their departure, a leaflet consisting of single A4 sheet, folded in three, thanking them for attendance and explaining a little about the church building and the Christian faith and suggesting they may care to return as a visitor or a worshipper at another time.

Mission statements

Organisations as diverse as supermarkets and hospitals, department stores and schools, display their mission statements. Followers of Jesus have been sent on a mission and many Churches have thought it a good thing to publish their own mission statement.

The first effect of a mission statement is to remind Church members of the task to which they are committed. It cannot be copied from anywhere else, as it relates directly to what God is saying to you in a unique situation of time and place. Because situations change the mission statement is not set for all time; it needs to be reviewed and possibly amended.

Followers of Jesus have been sent on a mission.

The second effect of your statement is the clear and concise statement it provides for all your visitors. The Cheshire Cat in *Alice in Wonderland* said, 'If you don't know where you're going, it doesn't matter which way you go.' We do know where we are going and there may be many reasons why we should say so in a mission statement.

Not all statements are as clear as they might be. The comic strip at dilbert. com gives an example:

Our mission is to enthusiastically network high-payoff benefits in order that we may professionally foster business meta-services to meet our customer's needs.

Martin Robinson, in *The Faith of the Unbeliever* (Monarch, 2001), writes:

In learning to communicate it will be important for the church to recognise the points of contact between the Christian message and a world for whom that message is unfamiliar and very foreign. At the heart of the Christian gospel lies a message of hope. One of the features of the exhausted west is the absence of hope. It is an absence which is so profound that any talk of hope seems foolish and empty.

Professional advisers suggest that a mission statement should consist of two or three sentences at the most. Firstly it should indicate your purpose or the reason for your ministry and the anticipated result of your ministry. Secondly it should outline the activities that will accomplish your purpose and thirdly it should indicate the beliefs that you share and are endeavouring to put into practice.

It has been suggested that the purpose should include an action and the object of the action, e.g. 'to reduce poverty'. The purpose is not the method but should indicate how things will change as a result of its implementation. Here is an example from a very dynamic Church which certainly needs a high level of drive and devotion to fulfil its mission:

God loves us and we wish to give that love to others by making our premises and ourselves available to the community and individuals within it. We believe that God is passionately concerned with the welfare of all people and the whole of his creation and we intend to share that passion.

Some texts that are called mission statements are really mottoes – which are very good in their own right but, again, care is needed. A motto, such as this one hung on the wall of a Christian coffee shop, might well remind the staff of the reason they are working there and the behaviour they wish to exhibit but their customers might not feel totally welcome!

Love God, Love each other and Love the lost.

Some questions to consider

- Can we list the different groups of people who come into our church outside Sunday?

- What clubs and organisations could we invite to use our church?

- Can those looking for help from specialist agencies find details in our church?

- Do we have a mission statement? Is it obvious to anyone who uses the church?

- Could there be a faith card on the seats when outside groups are using the church?

- Is there an eye-catching display of our Church programme, designed for visitors?

10

The Churchyard

Contributed by Brian Godfrey

It is rare to find a church that is not surrounded by some sort of open space. It may be a small paved area around an inner-city church or an extensive burial ground. Whatever it is, it will convey a message to the visitor.

Visitors

People visit churchyards for various reasons. Many will be visiting to tend the grave of a relative. Others will be looking at inscriptions to fill in details of a family tree. Yet others will just want a place to sit and reflect. It is not uncommon for churchyards to have a public footpath running through them. It is possible that even more visitors visit or pass through the churchyard than go into the church itself, so it is important to consider what message our churchyards are conveying. Is there any way you can enhance that message to give some spiritual significance? Maybe you can encourage people not just to visit the churchyard, but go into the church as well.

First impressions

First impressions of the church are often from the churchyard through which your visitor has to walk. Notice boards are referred to in elsewhere in this book but it is worth underlining that the notice boards outside the church are very important. They are probably the first things a visitor will see, after the church itself.

Notice boards vary in content but it would be strange not to have the name of the church. Many have the name of a contact and some have devised a system whereby the time of the next service can be shown. This is especially helpful where the services are irregular or infrequent.

Which door?

If there are several doors to the church, visitors need to be directed to the one that is open. It may be good to have a 'welcome notice' indicating that the church is open for visitors close to the gate. St Giles, Hooke in West Dorset has a notice showing whether the church is open or closed beside the main entrance but visible from the main gate. One church on the Romney Marshes in Kent has its 'church open' notice placed so that it is visible from the church car park.

Safe paths

What of the safety of your churchyard visitors? The path and verges leading to the main door are important and proper Christian concern can be exercised by warning if the path is uneven or, at times, slippery. Even if the rest of the churchyard has, for conservation reasons, long grass, neatly mown verges to the main path create an impression of care and welcome.

A rota of Saturday path-sweepers keeps the main approach to the church tidy.

One church in west Kent has a path lined by overhanging trees; a rota of Saturday path-sweepers keeps the main approach to the church tidy, and also free of leaves, moss and debris which might make it slippery when wet. What about a handrail if the path is steep or uneven? Indeed you might want to do a risk assessment for the whole of the churchyard. Are there any tombstones that are unstable and could be potentially dangerous?

Hiding clutter

Dustbins, watering cans, wheelbarrows and other things that are needed to maintain the churchyard should be tucked away out of sight of the main entrance.

Wildlife space

Churchyards have always been treated as special places. Consecration sets them apart for burials and makes them distinct from the surrounding land. This isolation means that they often have retained plants and animals in habitats which have been lost in the adjacent areas. This is particularly important in urban and suburban areas where most of the surrounding land has been built on and can be equally important in rural areas where past agricultural practices have reduced natural habitats for wildlife. Grassland in rural churchyards is often some of the most natural, having never been treated with fertilisers, pesticides and herbicides. These are wonderful areas to exercise Christian stewardship of the environment to encourage wildlife.

Over the last two or three decades the value of churchyards as conservation areas has been recognised and in many dioceses churches are encouraged to manage churchyards to sustain and encourage wildlife. The Diocese of Salisbury has a 'Living Churchyard' scheme in which participating churches have their churchyards judged by a panel of experts and awards are given on the basis of how they are managed for wildlife. All participating churches receive a certificate that can be displayed. It is an opportunity to involve the local community, especially any local schools, and this can be a means of bringing people within the orbit of the church.

However a churchyard is managed to encourage wildlife, there are likely to be areas where the grass is not mown until late in the year to permit wildflowers to grow. Where such management schemes are in place Churches are encouraged to use notices to explain their management plan and why certain areas of the churchyard are as they are. Notices need to be both discreet and

"IN THIS AREA IT'S THE ONLY HABITAT OF THE LESSING COURTING COUPLE"

legible. There is also an opportunity to link the Christian message of steward-ship of the environment to the management scheme. You could quote Psalm 24.1: 'The earth is the Lord's and all that is in it, the world, and those who live in it.' Through the beauty of nature we can make the link between the natural world and God who created it.

Through the beauty of nature we can make the link between the natural world and God who created it.

In one imaginative scheme in the churchyard at Beaminster in Dorset, a large area of grass was left unmown in the late spring to allow plants to flower and set seed. A series of narrow paths were cut as a maze leading, if the correct path was taken, to a cross in the middle. There are several ways of link-ing the idea of a maze with the Christian pilgrim-age towards Christ and the cross.

Quiet space

People visit churchyards for different reasons. Some may come just to find peace and quiet; a chance to find God in stillness. The provision of suitably placed benches is important for those who might want to spend time in such a place. If there is a footpath through the churchyard a bench might provide a convenient resting place for a weary walker. Other ideas for hospitality can be found in Chapter 3.

Those people who regularly visit graves need to be catered for. Areas for cremated remains and their associated memorials need to be neat and tidy. The same applies if there are parts of the churchyard that are still open for burials. Would it be helpful to remind people, by way of a carefully worded notice, that the church is open for prayer and that leaflets are available con-taining suitable prayers that they could use?

Temporary features

A number of churches, particularly where they have space and are in a prom-inent position, will create an Easter Garden or perhaps erect a cross for Good Friday. As with similar things inside the church building, a notice, readable at some distance, would remind people of the deeper significance.

"TRUE, IT'S NOT IDEAL
FOR PEACE AND QUIET"

"THEY'RE INSTALLING A LOOP
TO MAKE IT EASIER TO HEAR"

All too often cemeteries are thought of only as places of death and for the dead. Christians' profound belief in the resurrection means that somehow we need to make it clear that the churchyard is a place of hope as well. If your churchyard is well managed and lovingly tended the message it can convey is one of hope and encouragement.

You might consider opening your churchyard as part of the annual Open Gardens Scheme. It could present an opportunity to create some extra notices or a leaflet highlighting significant features in your churchyard, which you could link the Christian faith in some way. Equally it might provide an opportunity to encourage those visiting the churchyard to go into the church. As the Open Gardens Scheme operates only on certain days you could do some practical hospitality with refreshments on hand.

Some questions to consider

- Is our churchyard 'warm and welcoming' or is it formal or even uncared for?

- In what ways could our churchyard convey the gospel message of hope?

- How can we encourage visitors to the churchyard to go into the church?

- What pastoral ministry can we offer to people visiting relatives' graves?

- If there is or will be a conservation area, how can we help visitors appreciate it?

11

How to Do it – Further Ideas

This is a long chapter. You may care to read the general suggestions that follow but when it comes to specific ideas why not simply cast your eye over those of particular interest?

Presenting your church

These examples show the way in which various Churches have or might set about the task of offering information to their visitors. In the main, the Churches concerned are not named as many texts are not unique and can be found in different locations. You may like some ideas and not others; perhaps some words really appeal to you. If possible do not use them! Work on your own presentation and have what marketing people call a 'house style'. It can apply to the complete presentation, including layout, type-faces and the materials used. It is probable that the more costly the presentation, the longer will be its life and the better the look. The presentation of the message is important. Poor presentation could even result in a text being ignored. There are some longer texts in the examples. Be aware: too long, especially if poorly presented, and they will not be read at all. It's all down to your judgement. Many people are fond of their own work but critical of others'; why not make a point of looking at what has been done elsewhere? The criticism or appreciation of what you find may help you to evaluate your own work.

Hopefully you will find ways of engaging your visitors' attention other than by words but words are important. They generally need to be few and they need to be jargon free in order to be understood by those with no Christian upbringing. It really is worth saying again that it is good to have wording which will make sense to visitors who have no knowledge of the Bible or theology or church history. There is great mystery in our faith. It has to be so when we, weak and sinful creatures, are caught up by grace in God's plans and purposes. If at all possible do not add to that mystery by careless wording!

Before working on your own presentation, consider what you are trying to convey to your visitor. Think, for example, of baptism and the font. It may be made of stone or metal. It may be where it has always been or it may have been moved for a particular reason. You may have a portable font. It may have been built for total immersion of an infant but now contains a fruit bowl to hold the water. It may have a lid which was designed to keep out all sorts of nasties throughout the year in which the same water remained, 'protected' by salt and oil. The lid is now not functional, at least not for its original purpose, so should it be allowed to 'hide' the font? Westminster Cathedral has a font above ground which ranks between a mini swimming pool and an oversized jacuzzi. It carries a faith interpretation which reads:

> The font is large as a reminder of the days when baptism was always by immersion – a sign of our sharing in the death, burial and resurrection of Jesus Christ as our sins are washed away and we are spiritually reborn.

In your presentation you might decide that the meaning of what happens at baptism is more important than the frequently seen explanation as to why the font is octagonal, as some are.

Do you want to describe the materials used at a baptism or the event or the symbolism or its effect? Here are some ideas and words that might be used in one or other of those approaches:

Relating to the materials:
Water, words, clothes, candles, oil.
Relating to the event:
Get-together, family, Church, celebration, sacrament.
Relating to the symbolism:
Washing, refreshing, life, dying and rising, in Christ, darkness to light, joy, anointing.
Relating to the effect:
Initiation, welcome, membership, grace, new life, forgiveness.

You may care to make use of advice from the Plain English Campaign; it would certainly be advisable to ask a number of people to comment on your work before it is set in stone – although that is about the only presentational format you are unlikely to use! Be positive. Say that the church is open until 6 pm rather than the church will be closed at 6 pm. And ask yourself whether everything has to be in the style of a direct interpretation. Why not add a question or two to engage with your visitor or simply ask them to think about something? You could even leave them with a story to puzzle over – Jesus seemed to find that method quite useful!

Ideas to consider

❖ **Outside signs for the motorist to read**

The faster the road or the traffic on it, the larger the notice needs to be. Keep it clear and simple; you are aiming to notify, not to distract.

Open for You

Open for visiting and prayer

Church and car park open until dusk

❖ **Outside signs for the pedestrian**

Churches frequently use the word 'Welcome' and sometimes a variation on 'Do come in'. This is seldom seen on other buildings, whether commercial, historical or residential, all of which may be pleased to receive visitors, so is it something else which draws people in? It might be an open door; it could be the word, 'Free'.

This church is open. Visit today. A space to pray. Gifts and cards.

Coffee shop, book shop, meeting place. Mondays–Saturdays; 9.30–5.00

Nature in all its diversity grants us a glimpse into the heart of God the Father, which is nothing but love. Trust in his love and you will never be disappointed. (Found on the gate of a well planted rural churchyard)

On one of the boards you may think of using professionally produced posters, which are designed to communicate with those who are not members. See the Resources section for publishers.

❖ Main external notice board

Some of these boards are huge but most can only be read by a pedestrian or a slow driver. Some are on the pathway quite close to the building. As with everything else, there will be varying opinions on what should be displayed: what is important relating to the life of the Church as a centre for worship and what could be used to attract visitors. This board is the first opportunity for you to convey the really important information – and you must decide what that is. Remember that not everything has to be in the same size lettering.

The true treasure of this church is the good news that has been celebrated here for a thousand years: God loves us and wishes to bless us. Here is hope. Come in and learn more about this beautiful building.

Welcome to this ancient place of worship. Enjoy the history enshrined in these stones but also discover meaning, receive peace and find hope.

Welcome to this church where many worship God but others come to wonder, to enjoy our heritage, to ask questions. Whatever you have come for, you are welcome.

❖ Display boards

Commercially sourced boards are expensive but less expensive than possibly more aesthetically pleasing boards made especially for your church. Boards can be used for many types of display from overseas development to a timeline of local society; from the history of the Bible to the recent activities of your Church youth club. Many presentations will be suitable for Church member and visitor alike but others will be better if they are designed with one or the other in mind. The Monday to Saturday church can have a display placed where it might not be convenient for the worshipping community. As part of your welcome you might wish to have a country and a world map with a plentiful supply of pins together with an invitation to your visitor to indicate the location of their own home. If you do this then try to find a prominent place for it – perhaps towards the door, where it could be seen and used on the way out.

❖ Dog bowls

Well-behaved dogs on leads are welcome in this church.

❖ The porch and the door

This church is open today. Please come in.

Friend, you enter this church not as a stranger but as a guest of God. He is your heavenly father. Come then with joy in your heart and thanks on your lips into his presence, offering him your love and service. Be grateful to the strong and loyal men who in the name of Jesus Christ built this place of worship and to all who have beautified and hallowed it with their prayer and praise.

This is God's House. Be welcome here whoever you are; whether of this household or of another way, whether wanderers or deserters, be welcome.

❖ Money

Many Churches invite visitors to contribute towards not only the fabric but also the ministry of the Church. It is often a surprise to visitors that there is no state support or central funding for the building, which may be part of the nation's heritage. There is no harm in telling people. Nevertheless, you may think of both the ministry of the Church and the gospel as a free gift to your visitor. As the Lord said, 'freely you have received, freely give.' Research shows that most visitors wish to give, although you may think it is counter-productive to have notices such as the following which were the only form of welcome in the churches where they were displayed:

> It costs £194 per week to keep this beautiful church open. Any help you can give towards this cost would be very much appreciated and put to good use.

> Welcome to our church. Coming here as a visitor you are following the steps of those who have visited this place continuously for almost 1,000 years. Many left gifts to help the Church in its work – if you would like to do the same you will find an offertory box . . .

The receptacle in which the money is collected could be important. A Saxon church in Northumbria that receives a lot of American visitors simply has an open brass dish. There is no notice but it is placed near the door and is primed with $10 bills every morning!

❖ **Welcome, general**

Some churches say their welcome in up to 30 languages, either outside or inside. The exercise of discovering which language-groups of people visit your church could provide you with a welcoming opportunity.

> Rest here awhile and enjoy the serenity of this church, in the knowledge that God loves and cares for you and may the peace of Jesus Christ go with you.

> You are a visitor and an honoured guest. God knows your joys, he knows your sorrows. Be glad or be sad. Stand and stare, sit and be silent, kneel and know that you are welcome.

❖ Welcome table and welcome words

Try to find something that suits your building and the available space. Decide whether the welcome will be warmly personal or semi-official. Will the information be handwritten, computer-generated, or typeset? Will you use paper or card and will it be laminated or framed? Will the wording be black on white or coloured? Will you use logos, crests or pictures? The variety is endless.

We are glad you are visiting . . .

Please take this home as a reminder of your visit to . . .

There can be more than one welcome and those who habitually surf the net may even risk:

> Welcome. If you are used to surfing we regret that we cannot tell what number visitor you are but we can tell you that people have been hitting this site for the last 850 years – since when it has been involved in the World Wide Worship of Jesus Christ.

Perhaps you think it would be right to offer a greeting which is Christian in nature? For example something scriptural:

John 3.16: 'God so loved the world . . .'

1 Timothy 2.4: 'God wants all people to learn the truth.'

Matthew 11.28: 'Jesus said, "Come to me all who are weary and burdened".'

John 14.6: 'Jesus said, "I am the way, the truth and the life".'

Romans 1.7: 'Grace and peace to you from God our Father and from the Lord Jesus Christ.'

Or the greeting could be a declaration such as:

In the name of God we welcome you.

We have inherited this house of prayer and wish to share it with you.

The people of this Christian community greet you.

❖ The church guide

Visitors expect the church guide to be about the building and you will want to honour that, especially if they have paid for it. That means that although there will be a welcome in God's name and a note that the primary reason for the building is to enable people to worship God, you will quickly turn to interpreting the building. Of course you may still make reference to the faith, perhaps 'boxing' it against various items.

If the guide concludes with a reference to Christian faith there could also be an invitation to raise questions with someone in your own congregation or with an organisation such as the Christian Enquiry Agency or the Catholic Enquiry Office.

> Our faith is about feeling the love of God; it is knowing that each of us matters to him – that we are accepted and loved; it is about becoming, through Christ, nothing less than sons and daughters of God.

Some guides to the building contain a version of '*One Solitary Life*', the first recorded mention of which is within the sermon of a Canadian preacher in 1926, according to research recorded on the internet:

> Here is a man who was born in an obscure village, the child of a peasant woman. He worked in a carpenter's shop until he was thirty and then for three years he was an itinerant preacher. He had no credentials but himself. While still a young man, the tide of popular opinion turned against him.

His friends – the twelve men who had learned so much from him, and had promised him their enduring loyalty – ran away and left him. He went through the mockery of a trial; he was nailed on a cross between two thieves; when he was dead he was laid in a borrowed grave through the pity of a friend.

Yet I am well within the mark when I say that all the armies that ever marched, and all the parliaments that ever sat, and all the kings that ever reigned, put together, have not affected the life of man upon this earth as has this one solitary life.

❖ Children's guides

Many churches have guides for children. Most are no longer than four A5 pages and invite interaction by the writing of answers or the ticking of boxes. Some offer a prize. It is happily true that children's guides tend to allude to the faith far more frequently than adult guides, nevertheless they rarely seem to incorporate a direct message of God's love and care. If you have a children's guide you might consider whether a rewrite would be a good thing – this would not be the expensive exercise involved in rewriting the adult guide.

❖ Baptism

When writing about baptism you might want to check some biblical references:

Matthew 3.11; 28.19
Mark 1.9-11; 16.16
Acts 2.38, 41; 8.12ff.; 8.36ff.; 9.18; 10.38ff.; 16.15; 16.33; 18.8; 19.5; 22.16
Romans 6.3-4
1 Corinthians 12.13
Galatians 3.27
Ephesians 4.5
Colossians 2.12
1 Peter 3.21

This is the place of baptism. We are washed in the water of Life as we begin our eternal life in Christ, in whose death and Resurrection we believe and trust. Water is poured over the head three times, in the name of the Father, Son and Holy Spirit.

Hundreds of baptisms have taken place in our lovely ancient font. Baptism is the rite by which people become members of the Christian family. At baptism water from the font is poured over the person being baptised. Water is used because it symbolises washing and cleansing and is a sign that God promises to forgive us when we acknowledge and confess to God the things we have done wrong. Jesus was baptised himself and you can read about that in the Bible (Mark 1.9–11).

The following three paragraphs are from the children's church guide at Helmsley:

Jesus said all those being trained as his followers should be baptised. That is what happens here. Water is used to suggest washing away impurity; giving refreshment to the thirsty and a new life full of hope and confidence in God's love.

This special ceremony celebrates lots of things. It says thank you that the baby has been born safely and that mum is well. It says thank you for a new life, and for all the things that give life, such as water. It says thank you to God, who like a loving parent, wants to be our friend from the very start of our life and always take good care of us.

But water can be dangerous stuff – fast flowing rivers and treacherous seas can take life as well as give it. Having water at baptism also reminds us that in times of danger, even death itself, God will not let us go, but wants us to be with him for ever.

❖ **Stoup**

Those who have been baptised remind themselves that they belong to Jesus by dipping their finger in the water and marking themselves with the sign of the cross.

❖ Chancel step

Marriages take place here. We pray for God's blessing on them, we share their joy and celebrate their love.

❖ Altar

The large table at the front with six candles above it is called the altar. On the altar a special meal is prepared, reminding us of the meal eaten by Jesus and his friends on the night before he died. We pray that as we share in a similar meal, Jesus will be with us, his friends in this Church.

The night before his death Jesus sat down to a very special meal with his friends. We remember this every week as we stand in a circle round this table and share bread and wine to which Jesus gave a very special meaning, saying that they represented his life which he sacrificed for us.

This is the sanctuary with the altar. Here we remember Christ's death for us on the cross and our need to receive forgiveness and strengthening.

❖ Side chapels

Hereford cathedral uses a standard pattern with its descriptive material. The notices start with, 'As Christians we worship God ...' Each explanation concludes with an appropriate verse of scripture.

> As Christians we worship God whose goodness is seen in the lives of the saints. We give thanks for those who have walked with us on the way and are now at rest.
>
> At this place, for many centuries, men and women and children have prayed at the shrine of St Thomas of Hereford.
>
> 'With this great cloud of witnesses around us, therefore we too must throw off every encumbrance and the sin that all too readily restricts us and run with resolution the race which lies ahead of us, our eyes fixed on Jesus, the pioneer and perfecter of our faith.'

❖ Lectern

The lectern may be in the shape of an eagle (occassionally a pelican). The eagle is one of the symbols representing St John the Evangelist, author of the fourth Gospel. The association is either that the eagle was thought to be able to look at the sun and these words look into the unsurpassed brilliance of the heart of God or that the words of John are the most spiritually enlightened parts of the Bible and soar to the greatest heights. In your description of the use of the lectern you may wish to refer to the Bible as the book from which Christian faith is taught. Another option would be to quote well-known and everyday phrases that come from the Bible, probably to the surprise of your visitors. You could even produce a list to be taken away.

> **There is a Bible here. We call it the Word of God. It is the manual, the instruction book and the inspiration for Christian living.**

> From here we read the words of the Christian scriptures – the holy Bible – the word of God. It is in two parts: the Old Testament, the record of God's involvement with the people of Israel; and the New Testament, the good news of new life and hope in Jesus Christ.

❖ Pulpit

In the simple and straightforward way that you use to explain things, it might be as well to choose words other than 'preach' and 'sermon'.

> From here the reading from the Bible is thought through. This often challenges the way we behave but at the same time we are renewed in our faith and reminded of how God's Holy Spirit will help us every day.

> It is not easy to live a life that we are satisfied with, let alone one that pleases God. From this pulpit people are taught from the Bible – the book that outlines Jewish history, the life of Jesus and the early Church.

> From this pulpit the word of God is preached. The sermon seeks to interpret the scriptures for daily living: we listen to hear what God has to say to us.

❖ Lighting

Use well-placed and only selected lights, perhaps of the long-life variety – the cost is quite low and the rewards great, both for your visitors and your gift box.

> You are invited to switch on the lights but please remember to switch them off as well.

> The lights can be switched on by pressing this button as far as it will go. It is timed to switch the lights off after 15 minutes.

> The lights will come on automatically when you reach . . .

❖ Mission statements and similar commitments

Your mission statement informs a wider audience – your visitors – of your members' commitment. If it is to be meaningful to your visitors the wording needs to be in plain English.

> Our Parish Aim: To know God in and through his son Jesus Christ and make him more known through prayer in all its forms; learning and growing; and practical concern for the community.

> St ... exists to honour God, and to enable questioning, open-minded people to discover for themselves the significance of Jesus Christ.

> To be a community that loves Jesus and serves others in his name.

> Showing Jesus as Lord in our worship, witness, prayer and care.
> Celebrating God's grace,
> Expressing Jesus' love,
> Rejoicing in the Spirit's gifts,
> Spreading the Good News.

❖ Easter garden

Many Easter gardens are lovingly created mini works of art. And yet although they might be meaningful to the congregation they do not speak for themselves. As this is one area where visitors might pause for a moment, consider displaying a full explanation well laid out on an A4 card.

> Do you know the story behind this beautiful garden? Jesus was put to death by being nailed to a cross. At the same time two other people were put to death because of the bad things they had done. That is why there are three crosses. Jesus had never done anything bad; he healed people and he taught them about God but the rulers in his country thought he would take over as a popular leader. To put him to death was the best way to stop that happening. He died on a Friday (we call it Good Friday) and was buried in a tomb (a small cave). Three days later (counting Friday, Saturday, Sunday) he was raised from the dead. That was the first Easter. The stone blocking his tomb was rolled away to show that he was no longer there. A man who was dead is now alive! We believe Jesus died to enable every person to get back to God from whom we are separated. We believe God raised Jesus from the dead and gave him life again (we call it the resurrection) because Jesus had taken our sin on himself so that we could again become friends with God. To become God's friends, all we have to do is to trust in the living Jesus.

❖ Invitation to pray

All the work you are doing is for the benefit of your visitors to whom even an invitation to pray might sound either a little presumptive or slightly aggressive. If your invitation was simply to sit and pause or even to rest, your visitor might feel under less obligation and feel it easier to spend time in the area provided. This was why it was suggested that an easy chair might not be out of place – unless in your prayer area it would be aesthetically unsuitable.

A sign with the words, 'If you wish to pray' or 'If you wish to be quiet' could point your visitor to the prayer area. Although many may know what a chapel or a crypt is, there is no need to use these particular words which may be strange to some. Simply ensure that the signing is clear, whether from a distance or at the place of prayer itself.

❖ **Prayer requests**

Where visitors are invited to leave prayers – such as on a prayer board or prayer tree or in a prayer box – it would be courteous to have an indication of what will happen to the prayers: when and where they will be used by praying people and how long they will remain where they have been placed. For example:

> Prayers are offered regularly in Church and requests are particularly included in our Sunday evening services at 6 pm and Friday prayers at 12 noon. Please date requests – they are removed after about a month. Thank you for praying with us.

Would it be good to encourage visitors to give thanks as well as making requests for assistance or blessing? Perhaps you could provide a separate board for prayers of thanksgiving.

❖ **Prayer aids**

This is one area in which you may, with advantage, use what others have prepared. There are prayers in the worship books you use and there are many anthologies of prayers that you could consult. It is a matter of selection and then presentation – bearing in mind the constraints of copyright. Books, cards, leaflets, and papers can all be used. Will you rotate the prayers you have on offer according, say, to either the Church calendar or the seasons of the year? Will you regularly provide topical prayers and will you provide prayers that are related to personal grief and sorrow, joy and gladness?

As well as set prayers, why not provide a list of Bible passages that might be helpful? If you wish to do this it is a matter of deciding whether to print the Bible passage in full or to provide a Bible for the passages to be found – it would be helpful if you marked or highlighted the passages.

❖ Candles

Words to accompany the lighting of candles can be on a display or on smaller cards for visitors to take with them – or both.

> We utter our prayer but it does not die on our lips.
> Offer your prayer to God and leave it with him:
> For someone who needs your prayers and needs God
> For the world of conflict and pain
> For yourself that you might bring love and hope to others.

> A candle:
> A sign of our prayer and the offering of our lives.
> A reminder to us and to others of the saints and martyrs who have shone as lights of the world and who pray for us.
> A witness to all who pass by that this is a place of prayer.

> The large candle you see here is lit for the first time at Easter and then again every time there is a baptism. Candles have often been used as a symbol of Jesus, who called himself 'the light of the world'.

❖ Stained glass windows

As mentioned earlier, it is helpful to place a photograph of the window low enough for children to read, together with an appropriate interpretation. An alternative would be a text accompanied by a line drawing and an invitation to take it to a place in the church where the window can easily be seen in its entirety.

❖ 'Take me' card

A small (2½ in x 4 in) card with a drawing of the church on the front and the words, 'Take me with you' could be at the font or lectern or altar – as considered appropriate – to remind your visitors of something that has been said in that place, about God and about us. For example, the card at the font could have a drawing of your font and say:

> Life depends on water. The water at the font talks about new life that God will give me.

The card at the altar may say:

> Life depends on bread. The bread given at the altar talks of food for life that God will give me.

❖ A relevant faith – the wayside pulpit

Those who are prepared to comment on current affairs from a faith perspective may frequently find high profile news items that could be used to make a bridge from life as it is to life as God offers. These 'Headlines for the week' could be posted on a board reserved for that purpose inside or outside the church. A tough job, unless it was an extract from last week's sermon!

The wayside pulpit, using that as a generic term rather than referring to the posters published under that name, may have more relevance to a believer than to a non-believer. You will need good judgement in choosing what is suitable. The November poster, 'Come early and avoid the Christmas rush' has, at least, the benefit of showing that the church houses a living congregation. You will have to decide the gospel impact that such artwork may have on a visitor – or even on someone who simply looks from afar. Even a church that does not open its doors during the week could have leaflets in a container by the gate or porch that say why the church is there and what it has to offer. People are naturally curious and leaflets would be taken. Some people are also very untidy, so it might be responsible to check at least once a day that the leaflets are not decorating the church path or the public pavement.

❖ School visits

Schools are likely to include visits to churches for a range of curricular purposes: history, geography, arts, science, and religious education. There are references to visits to places of worship at all Key Stages. Then Secretary for State for Education Charles Clarke, launching the national framework for religious education in 2004, said: 'Faith groups must seize this opportunity to develop their own resources that enhance understanding of their faith, and their response to world issues. I support the development of materials that can be used with the framework.'

This does not mean that a teacher with prepared material and a tight schedule will welcome your enthusiastic interruption! What it does mean is that you have good reason to approach local schools offering your church for their use. Teachers will make return visits if you are able, for example, to deliver fascinating insights into interesting local people who have been baptised and married in your church and perhaps moving onto burial and books of remembrance, headstones and flowers at anniversaries. While observing approved precautions and parental permissions, let the children play the organ, ring the bells and change the seasonal cloths on the altar. Check beforehand that there will be time for squash and biscuits. Tell them about the love of God and the friendship of Jesus.

❖ Weddings, baptisms, thanksgivings, dedications, funerals, memorial services

By their nature these services, together with other celebrations, will always attract people who are not regular worshippers and often people from outside the neighbourhood. There will frequently be a Christian address, hymns, prayers and Bible readings and so your visitor will be well exposed to the faith and you may think that is enough. At the end of the service a few people may look around but most will leave immediately as the gathering is often continued elsewhere.

On these occasions many churches do not remove the gift aid envelopes or the welcome cards which are normally found on the seats or pew ledges. Might it be more appropriate to substitute a small double-sided card carrying words of thanksgiving, sorrow, joy, and hope, as appropriate to the particular service, with an invitation to take it away?

> Please take this card. It will remind you that today God has played a part in your life.

❖ World Wide Web

This book is about something very down to earth, namely your church building and the use you are making of it in telling visitors about your faith. They have come to you and you have engaged with them. You have welcomed them physically.

However, more and more people are searching the web before going somewhere – even before going nowhere! All that you have prepared for your Monday to Saturday congregation could be made available for web surfers.

A search on Google, made as this book was being written, indicated there were 51 million pages in response to the word 'God' – with a site called 'Does God exist?' as the first listed. There were 53 million pages offered in response to the word 'church' and 22 million on the word 'spiritual'. It seems a lot of people are interested in these words.

Broadly speaking there are three varieties of site relating to churches. The first are directories comprising lists indicating church location and when services are held. The second cover sites published by an individual Church for its own purposes. The information on these is most often addressed to its own congregation.

The third type of site are related either to specialist areas such as bells or stained glass or churches with round towers. A large number of these sites are devoted to describing, with pictures, the inside and outside of churches. As an example you could look at Simon Knott's labour of love which features 645 churches in Suffolk alone – www.suffolkchurches.co.uk. Sites like these will increasingly bring visitors to your church and can be used, in their own right, as a way of communicating God's love. To build a site that offers a virtual tour of your church requires an amount of skill, flair and software but the style that Simon Knott has used demands no greater expertise than some people in your own church might already demonstrate when creating their own sites to contain family archives.

Whatever type of site you build, remember that many of those who visit it may know little about the God we worship. More and more churches are providing an opportunity for people to explore faith by putting a link on their home page to such websites as www.rejesus.co.uk. This is a site produced on behalf of churches in Britain and Ireland. It offers the opportunity to explore Jesus Christ, his followers and what Christian faith means today. Banners can be downloaded for church sites from the 'About us' section of www. rejesus.co.uk. Of course, there are many more sites that you might think are suitable.

As old computers are often thrown away you could easily acquire one to have running in your church in order to show your own website. Little security would be necessary and for this purpose it would not have to be connected to the web. You could also download onto the hard disc some other

Christian sites and make them available to your visitors. Those who stop to look at the computer tour will be inspired to do the real thing. The opening screen could lead to a section for children: ideally this would be interactive.

❖ Farewell

Learning by extension is very popular these days. Travel and accommodation costs are avoided and learning can take place at the convenience of the student. Although your visitor is leaving the building there is every reason why you should encourage the experience to continue. And so if you didn't offer them at the welcome table, why not have available at the exit bookmarks with a picture of your church or some memorable feature and a prayer or a Bible text, together with a very limited indication of where they can learn more, certainly about God's love and perhaps about the buildings built to his glory?

Thank you for visiting St . . .

A notice at the exit:

Please visit us again.

A free offer of a plant or local produce:

We would like you to have one of these plants – do take one with you.

Preferably label it with its name and perhaps growing instructions. Why not also include a text that can be easily understood?

12

The Ministry of Welcome

Welcome and hospitality have been mentioned many times. Why, then, a chapter on the ministry of welcome, especially as this book is primarily written for those churches that are not hosted?

There are two reasons. Firstly is what could be called cross-fertilisation. If ideas that are suitable for unhosted churches can be applied where there is a

"THAT'S CLEAR"

"BUT HOW DO YOU GET IN?"

ministry of welcome, then unhosted churches may like to know what further benefits visitors might derive from being welcomed personally. Secondly you may not feel totally comfortable with what could seem to be nothing but a multiplicity of written notices. It is true that if every suggestion was followed there would be so many notices, explanations, illustrations and displays there may not even be enough room for your visitors! Use much of what has been recommended but not all at once. Revisit, review, renew, reconsider, rework; but please, never do it and then leave it as your gift to posterity.

A notice in one church reads:

> Along with many Churches the community of . . . tries to bear witness to the grace, passion, love, anger, tenderness and acceptance of Christ.

This is followed by an expression of the way that particular Church thinks it right to offer itself to its visitors, supported by a quotation from the monk and mystic Thomas Merton. It reads like this:

> We consider the priority 'is not so much to speak of Christ as to let him live in us that people might find him by feeling how he lives in us'.

This is an enormous challenge and is a lot more difficult than writing a notice or displaying a text. If this is to be your way in relation to your open church and the welcoming of visitors, you may well think that your first act of the day should be to join together in prayer. When consulted about the aims of this book an Archdeacon wrote:

Above all, it comes down to that indefinable sense of 'atmosphere'. We know it when we find it, but it is almost impossible to define. I think that what we need to do is to take praying in our churches much more seriously. There are some Christians who would say that regular committed praying in a church changes the atmosphere of a church. If we are serious about our ministry to visitors we need to commit ourselves to pray regularly in our churches. I know of one group who regularly met to pray in their church on a Saturday morning and who would say that the atmosphere of the church changed. It became more peaceful and it became easier to pray in.

The necessity for, and the centrality of prayer will not come as a surprise to those who have been committed to mission. While keeping an eye open for their visitors, your welcomers could be encouraged to continue praying throughout the day.

Where are the welcomers?

It is not difficult to hear the plaintive cry, 'We don't have enough people.' Before finding the people it may help to have a little inspiration. Rotherham Churches Tourism Initiative comprises 13 churches of varying sizes. They have recruited over 300 volunteers to church-sit. It is true that some Churches will have few members of their congregations who are of a suitable age and at home during the day. What is not often recognised is that there are people who are not Church members who have much goodwill for the church and pride in their heritage and who, if asked, might be pleased to help to keep 'their' church open. These folk will not be able to contribute to the faith interpretation but they could enable you to keep the building open, if that is the only way you can have a Monday to Saturday church.

> *They have recruited over 300 volunteers to church-sit.*

What will they do?

It is a 'ministry of welcome' but that does not mean being overbearing, gushing or too enthusiastic. A gentle, warm, smiling greeting and a willingness to help will not be far wrong. What you will need to decide is the extent of their brief. No doubt a watchful eye is necessary as, perhaps suggested by Proverbs 15.3: 'The eyes of the Lord are in every place, keeping watch on the evil and the good.' A better text might be two verses earlier: 'A soft answer turns away wrath, but a harsh word stirs up anger.'

Welcoming is not about the interpretation of the building and it would therefore not be appropriate to equate a welcomer with those often most excellent volunteers in National Trust properties. Nevertheless, visitors will expect your welcomers to know about the building and its unique aspects; ideally they will be able to talk with authority. It would be wonderful if

"YOU NEVER CAN BE TOO CAREFUL"

they were also able to talk of their own faith with certainty – and humility – but bear in mind a visitor may respond warmly to a 30-second personal testimony yet be a very uncomfortable recipient of a three-minute lecture in theology. If the flower arranger or the person who is polishing the brass has a few prepared words, which are part of their own faith story, they may themselves grow in confidence – as well as being a great help to your visitors. If there is an offer to pray with anyone who asks, make it easy for the appropriate person to be found without everyone else in the building being alerted to what is going on.

Training

Training to be a church welcomer is provided by many diocese and other Church bodies. Excellent courses are run by the Yorkshire Tourist Board and also by the Church Tourism Network Wales. They are based on a government-sponsored programme called Welcome Host which has been tailored for churches. The programme covers everything required, apart from faith-sharing. The course is normally fitted into one day but it does take the whole of 6 hours. The trainers from Wales will travel to you; they will need accommodation and their travel expenses will have to be reimbursed. There are certificates of accreditation for participants.

Training directly related to the telling of the good news of Jesus, comes under the heading of evangelism which this book does not cover but for which there are many existing books and courses.

Some questions to consider

- Can we draw up, publish and regularly review a brief for welcomers?

- Professional training pays dividends. What course might we use?

- Could we find welcomers among the local non-church community?

- How will we care for our welcomers? How often will we meet together?

- How can we ensure our welcomers do not have to suffer abuse?

- Are our cleaners, flower arrangers, etc. given information to help visitors?

"IT'S THE FIRST TIME THIS MONTH THAT ANYONE HAS ASKED FOR PRAYER"

13

Spirituality

We have all heard the words, 'I can worship God on the golf course as well as I can in church,' or 'I am never closer to God than when wandering along the riverbank.' It is not our task to judge such comments. If they are true for any person then we may be able to rejoice with them. Even so, we are unlikely to recommend that our Sunday congregation meets at the club house instead of the church or that each member takes an individual walk in preference to joining in corporate worship.

To avoid a possible rejoinder let us agree that it is possible for the Church to meet in the club house and individuals on the riverbank could be joined in a web church via their mobile phone but this book is about the church building in which the traditional Church meets!

The reference to Susan Howatch in the first chapter illustrates that we do not know where the road to Christian faith starts for any individual. A sunset, the death of a friend, a dream, the generosity of a stranger or the prayer of a grandmother; any event may be the starting point. We read that the building had a profound effect on Susan Howatch but we do not know if that was where her search began and there is certainly no reason to suppose she came to a personal faith in Jesus solely because of the beauty of the cathedral.

Christian faith, faith in God as Father, Son and Holy Spirit, is what theologians call a revealed religion. There is no suggestion that anyone can guess their way to God, despite the evidence all around us of a wonderful creation or a beautiful and prayed-in church. St Paul wrote that God's eternal power and divine nature had been evident for all to see but he did not suggest looking for God by any means other than considering the historic facts of the death and resurrection of Jesus. Paul had plenty of spiritual experiences but he didn't teach from those experiences; rather he instructed the young Church about what he had learned. He and the other New Testament writers majored on what is taken in through the mind, albeit perceived spiritually.

If we are going to use our buildings to convey the good news of God, then we need to interpret what happens within them. Within Christian faith 'spiritual' must refer to what is moved, directed and enabled by the Holy Spirit of God. Not only are Christians led by the Spirit of God they are also indwelt by the Spirit. Something has happened. Our own spirit is now not simply struggling, searching for something to complete or fulfil our humanity; our spirit is working with God's Spirit, who reveals God's love and purpose to us and in us.

The BBC television news reported the summer solstice celebrations of pagans at Stonehenge and Glastonbury. Their activities were described as 'spiritual' and then, with great perception, the reporter related spirituality in Christians to the Holy Spirit of God. A month later, on the occasion of the Church of England's Synod vote on the subject of women bishops, the BBC news again compared Church with other spiritual activity. Within that telecast a meditation centre spokesperson said that they 'aim to connect people with the spiritual part of their lives that church services no longer do' and 'there is more to spiritual life than the old image of God'. The camera moved from people dancing in a field to unite themselves with nature, to a church. The reporter said of the church, 'the Spirit here is the Holy Spirit; the part of God that Christians believe inhabits the world and inhabits people.' Not the way a theologian might put it but crystal clear in noting that the word 'spiritual' needs to be defined. We must do better than simply aiming to give people a good spiritual experience.

Jesus addressed his hearers as evil, which doubtless caused great offence. All that is bad in human action must surely qualify for the word 'spiritual' as well as all that is good and attractive. Christians, of all people, should recognise this, for they claim to fight against spiritual powers. The existence of spirituality on both sides of the moral divide is well illustrated in Acts 26, where Paul recalls the commission he received from Jesus when he was converted on the road to Damascus. He was to go to the Gentiles 'to open their eyes so that they may turn from darkness to light and from the power of Satan to God, so that they may receive forgiveness of sins and a place among those who are sanctified by faith in me.'

'Spiritual' is also a term frequently attached to works of art, of whatever medium. This poem, that picture, we are told, has a spiritual quality. If *ET* has a spiritual quality then presumably *The Exorcist* does as well. What about Picasso's cubism or Tracey Emin's bed? In the light of that, what should we make of the educationalist's recommendation to encourage children to paint in order to express their spirituality? If nothing else, it surely indicates the folly of equating 'spirituality' with Christianity. So what of Christian artists and craftsmen, composers and poets, who dedicate their talents to the glory of God? They have to find how to communicate in ways that help others to understand not just the spiritual but the spiritual which is derived from and points to God.

Hundreds of books have been written about spirituality and many others about sacred space. Most of them may be worth reading to gain insights as to how people behave and react; which is another way of saying how they are human or, confusingly, in today's jargon, how they are spiritual.

And so, to come back to your visitors: they are people we believe to have been made in the image of God, spiritual beings. We do not need to know what good or evil influences have affected their spirituality; we simply wish to be hospitable, welcoming and sympathetic to every visitor. We would neither tell them that they are seeking an encounter with the divine, as some Christian writers claim on their behalf, nor suggest that they are lost souls. Nevertheless, your own faith may well convince you that there is truth in Augustine's claim that there is a God-shaped hole in every heart that only God can fill and that is why you are engaging in an endeavour to present the Christian faith. That is why you are taking a God-given opportunity to share his love with your visitors and that is why you refer to the God we worship and not to some vague spirituality that could be found in an Eastern shrine or in a course on Gaia – or on the golf course. You are proclaiming the good news of Jesus in a building that was built to house a Christian Church and you are proclaiming it in a way that specifically and clearly relates to 'the faith that was once for all entrusted to the saints' (Jude 1.3).

Thoughts and closing questions

- All the senses may be actuated by a church visit. Music or warmth, lighting or fragrance might make people feel good and help them to be receptive. Space, colours, design and a certain smell might heighten awareness. All these things and many others might be thought of as spiritual but can they, by themselves, introduce our visitors to God? How will we try to ensure that the visitors to our church building not only learn of the love of God but also that he or she can receive God's love for themselves?

Resources

The author has attempted to check everything mentioned and would appreciate information on any incorrect details for amendment in future editions. The following abbreviations are used:

AL Authentic Lifestyle, the books of Paternoster Press. www.paternoster-publishing.com

AP Alpha Publications, Holy Trinity Brompton, Brompton Road, London SW7 1JA 0845 6447544 publications@htb.org.uk www.alpha.org.uk

ARC Acora Publishing, Arthur Rank Centre, Stoneleigh Park, Warwickshire CV8 2LZ 024 7685 3060

BB Bridge-builders (PTL UK), Vision Building, 4 Footscray Road, Eltham, London SE9 2TZ 020 8850 0111 ptl@zetnet.co.uk www.bridge-builders.net

CWR Crusade for World Revival, Waverley Abbey House, Farnham, Surrey GU9 8EP 01252 784710 www.everydaywithjesus.com

BP Bessacarr Prints, Thackray House, 42 Manor Road, Doncaster DN7 6SD 01302 351112

CAN Churches Advertising Network www.churchads.org.uk

CEA Christian Enquiry Agency, 27 Tavistock Square, London WC1H 9HH 020 7387 3659 cea@christianity.org.uk www.christianity.org.uk

CEO Catholic Enquiry Office, 114 West Heath Road, London NW3 7TX 020 8458 3316 enquiries@life4seekers.co.uk www.life4seekers.co.uk

CD Concept Design, 144a Ferry Road, Edinburgh EH6 4NX 0131 554 0339

CHP Church House Publishing, Great Smith Street, London SW1P 3NZ 020 7898 1451 www.chpublishing.co.uk

CIS Christians in Sport, Frampton House, Victoria Road, Bicester, Oxon OX26 6PB 01869 255630 info@christiansinsport.org.uk www.christiansinsport.org.uk

CP Canterbury Press, St Mary's Works, St Mary's Plain, Norwich NR3 3BH 01603

612914 www.scm-canterburypress.co.uk orders@scm-canterburypress.co.uk

CPO Christian Publishing and Outreach Ltd, Garcia Estate, Canterbury Road, Worthing, West Sussex BN13 1BW 01903 264556 enquiries@cpo.org.uk www.cpo.org.uk

DG Deo Gloria Resources, Freepost WC2947, South Croydon CR2 8UZ 020 8651 6246 resources@deo-gloria.co.uk www.deo-gloria.co.uk

ECP Evangelism & Church Planting, Methodist Church House, 25 Marylebone Road, London NW1 5JR 020 7467 5243

H & T Hunt & Thorp, Bowland House, off West Street, Alresford, Hampshire SO24 9AT

GB Grove Books Ltd, Ridley Hall Road, Cambridge CB3 9HU 01223 464748 www.grovebooks.co.uk

GBC The Good Book Company, Elm House, 37 Elm Road, New Malden, Surrey KT3 3HB 0845 225 0880 admin@thegoodbook.co.uk www.thegoodbook.co.uk

IBSUK International Bible Society UK, 3 Howard Buildings, 69/71 Burpham Road, Guildford GU4 7LX 01483 306869 www.eurobible.net/shop/uk/

IVP Inter-Varsity Press (United Kingdom), UCCF Book Centre, Norton Street, Nottingham NG7 3HR 0115 9781054 sales@ivpbooks.com

K Kingsway Publications, Lottbridge Drove, Eastbourne, East Sussex BN23 6NT 01323 437700 www.kingsway.co.uk

LW Lifewords (formerly Scripture Gift Mission). Lifewords materials are strictly for giving away. They are delivered with a note stating the value of the goods. Lifewords is also able to supply a display rack. 5 Eccleston Street, London SW1W 9LZ 020 7730 2155 contact@lifewords.info www.lifewords.info

M McCrimmons Publishing Ltd, 10–12 High Street, Great Wakering, Essex SS3 0EQ 01702 218956 www.mccrimmons.com

MC Methodist Church House, 25 Marylebone Road, London NW1 5JR 020 7486 5502

MU The Mothers Union, Mary Sumner House, 24 Tufton Street, London SW1P 3RB

ND Norwich Diocesan House, 109 Dereham Road, Easton, Norwich NR9 5ES 01603 880853

NLP New Life Publishing Company, PO Box 777, Nottingham NG11 6ZZ 0115 921 7280 sales@newlifepublishing.co.uk www.newlifepublishing.co.uk

OCT Open Churches Trust, c/o The Really Useful Group Ltd, 22 Tower Street, London, WC2H 9TW 020 7240 0880 oct@reallyuseful.co.uk www.openchurchestrust.org.uk

PB&M Pauline Books & Media, Middle Green, Slough, Bucks SL3 6BS 01753 577629

PT The Philo Trust, 141 High Street, Rickmansworth WD3 1AR 01923 772288 admin@philotrust.com www.philotrust.com

Plain English Campaign www.plainenglish.co.uk

RUN Reaching the Unchurched Network, PO Box 387, Aylesbury HP21 8WH 0870 7873635 info@run.org.uk www.run.org.uk

SU Scripture Union 207–209 Queensway, Bletchley, Milton Keynes, Bucks MK2 2 EB 01908 856000 www.scriptureunion.org.uk

StAD Stewardship Dept, Diocese of St Albans, Holywell Lodge, 41 Holywell Hill St Albans AL1 1HE 01227 854532 mail@stalbansdioc.org.uk

TNC The National Society for Promoting Religious Education and Church House Publishing, Church House, Great Smith Street, London SW1P 3NZ 020 7898 1518 enquiries@natsoc.c-of-e.org.uk www.natsoc.org.uk

TT Tim Tiley Ltd, 33 Zetland Road, Redlands, Bristol BS6 7AH 0117 9423397 sales@timtiley.com www.timtiley.com Tim Tiley is also able to supply display racks and stands and an introductory offer.

TTB Torch Trust for the Blind, Torch Way, Northampton Road, Market Harborough, Leicestershire LE16 9HL 01858 438260 info@torchtrust.org www.torchtrust.org

UCB PO Box 255, Stoke-on-Trent ST4 8YY 0845 6040401 www.ucb.co.uk/ inspirational UCB is a Christian media ministry within the UK and Ireland formed to promote the good news of the kingdom of God.

VAV Viz-A-Viz, info@vizaviz.org www.vizaviz.org

VCM Verité CM, 307 Tarring Road, Worthing, West Sussex BN11 5JG 01903 241975 enquiries@veritecm.com www.veritecm.com

Literature that can be customised for your locality

Which Way. An attractive and unique leaflet for the spiritual pilgrim that points the way towards faith in Jesus Christ. What is unique is that the leaflet is produced in a standard format but you complete it by supplying local photographs to earth the leaflet in the place where you are. It unfolds to eight panels of A6. CD

Look at . . . An A4 size eight-page illustrated guide to a particular church done in two colours in a comic book style that will appeal especially to children doing projects but certainly not childish. If there is a story connected with your church then so much the better. BP

Eye-catching leaflets to interest the casual browser

Life Issues Contact Cards. A range of four cards covering the issues of stress, love, forgiveness and satisfaction, offering a Bible verse, thought-provoking words and a free booklet from Christian Enquiry Agency. LW, DG

Angels and Nature. Postcards and packs of cards, aimed at those seeking spiritual fulfilment and offering practical thoughts about a harmonious and meaningful life. They introduce the spirituality of Jesus and the Bible and suggest ways for further investigation. Created by Bruce Stanley in conjunction with Christian Enquiry Agency. DG

Check it out. A small leaflet inviting people to check out God, covering freedom, fact or fiction, forgiveness and faith. VAV

What's your passion? A very small fold-out booklet which relates what we may be passionate about to discovering a relationship with God who is passionate about us. DG

What is a Catholic? A brief explanation of the Catholic Church including quotations from people about their faith, an invitation to www.life4seekers. co.uk and a response form for information from the Catholic Enquiry Office. CEO

Lord of Lords. Designed around cricket, this is just one of a wide selection of themed, excellently designed eight-fold A6 size leaflets that would appeal to sports people, travellers, steam buffs, environmental anoraks and many more besides. Around 100 titles to choose from. Catalogue available. CD

Why go to Church? A simple, small-size, three-panel leaflet giving reasons why people still attend Church. ND

What Christians Believe. An A4 two-fold leaflet that outlines basic Christian beliefs. ND

Christian Enquiry Agency (CEA)

Churches can put the Agency contact details on literature for visitors. This is provided confidentially – no follow up unless requested but further help is offered, including with a local Christian. CEA is an agency of Churches Together in Britain and Ireland. CEA

Outreach newspapers

Challenge. VCM
The Son. CPO
New Life. NLP

Outreach cards

A range of outreach cards and booklets are available that can be overprinted with local information. CPO

Guides

Pitkin Guides. Healey House, Dene Road, Andover, Hampshire SP10 2AA
Pilgrim Guides. Canterbury Press. CP

Prayer anthologies

Celtic Praise. Prayers of praise from Cornwall. By Pat Robson. TT
Celtic Reflections. These reflections shed a 'Celtic' light on such things as spirituality, the pilgrimage of life, creation, the home, community and other aspects of life. By Martin Wallace. TT
Celtic Prayer. By David Adams. Introduction and one prayer for each day of the week. TT
Who Cares? Thoughts and prayers for those who care and those who need care. Edited and compiled by Mary Oakley. TT
Living a Day at a Time. A seven-day prayer cycle especially for people following a bereavement. Edited and compiled by Mary Oakley. TT
In Quietness and Confidence. Quotations and prayers to help those who are growing older and experiencing loneliness. Edited and compiled by Mary Oakley. TT
Beyond the Gate. A collection of thoughts and prayers for those who have experienced the loss of a child. Edited and compiled by Mary Oakley. TT
Thoughts on Life to Come. A collection of thoughts and prayers that reflect on what happens beyond death. Edited and compiled by Mary Oakley. TT
God's Space in You. This booklet, in the 'Everyday Spirituality' series, would be very helpful in engaging people who are into 'spirituality' but who have not explored one that is focused on Jesus. H & T
Labyrinths and Prayer Stations. By Ian Tarrant and Sally Dakin. Grove Books. GB
How to Pray in Hospital. A guide for patients. By Barbara Haynes. MU

Additional sources of materials for prayer and devotional reading

Fairacres Publications. From SLG Press. CP
Kevin Mayhew Publications www.kevinmayhew.com
Redemptorist Publications. www.shineonline.net

Bible reading aids

For adults
Every Day with Jesus. Also available in large print. CWR
Word for Today. UCB
Daily Bread. SU
Encounter with God. SU
Grow with the Bible. www.grow-with-the-Bible.org.uk
Bible Alive. www.biblealive.co.uk
Bible Reading Fellowship Notes. www.brf.org.uk

For teenagers
YP's. CWR
Word 4U 2Day. UCB
One Up. For ages 11–14. SU

For children
Topz. CWR
Snapshots. For ages 8 –10. SU
Tiddlywinks. For under 5s. SU

Booklets on the basics of Christianity

Why Jesus? Nicky Gumbel explains that Christianity is about relationships and
  explores why Jesus came. There are cartoons and a prayer of commitment in
  this 20-page booklet. There's also a *Why Christmas?* version. AP
Journey into life. New edition of the booklet by Norman Warren exploring what
  is a Christian, sin, why Jesus came and the way ahead. K
Spelling it Out . . . about being a Christian. Subtitled 'An ordinary churchgoer
  offers to explain', this little booklet began life as a series of leaflets written by
  Kate Rhodes for visitors to Bolton Abbey. TT
The Light of the World. This little booklet has Holman Hunt's famous painting
  on the cover and gives the background story and an application of the message
  to our lives. By Dr Eric Hayden. TT
Christianity. A pocket-sized fold-out guide giving a brief overview of the Bible,
  answering questions about the Christian faith and including a prayer of
  commitment. GBC
Easter Sonrise. A message that goes right to the heart of Good Friday and Easter,
  attractively presented and written in a popular style by evangelist J. John. PT
The Life – A Portrait of Jesus. An easily read 250-page book on the life and
  significance of Jesus Christ for Christian and serious enquirer alike.
  Recommended for the book stall. By J. John and Chris Walley. AL

Christianity for the Open Minded. An excellent small booklet to engage the inquirer. There are other titles in the series that are well worth considering of which the following is a random selection. IVP

The Evidence for the Resurrection.

Are all Religions One?

Jewishness of Jesus.

Forgiveness.

Prayer.

Explaining worship

Tufton tracts. A4 cards that explain, 'What we do and why'. Titles are 'Making the sign of the cross', 'Anointing with oil', 'Genuflecting and bowing', 'Incense', 'Lighting a candle', 'Asking the prayers of the Saints'. CP

Booklets for giving away

Why me? A beautifully illustrated booklet for people who feel troubled. LW

Living with Loss. Reflections and Bible verses reproduced over beautiful scenes and images in a 24-page booklet for those recently bereaved. LW

Walking in the Desert. For those experiencing stress. A booklet with a message of rest, hope, restoration and strength. LW

Meditations of Life. A thoughtful booklet with meditations for those seeking spiritual answers to life. LW

Daily Strength. A collection of Bible verses and the Lord's Prayer alongside scenes and images in a 40-page small booklet. LW

The Little Book of Help. Some carefully selected biblical texts on a whole range of matters such as ambition, money, worry, relationships, friends, sex, rest, posssessions, etc. LW

The Little Book of Character. Carefully selected biblical texts on courage, loyalty, discipline, integrity, selfless commitment and respect for others. Produced originally with members of the armed forces in mind. LW

The Little Book of Life. Carefully selected biblical texts on the central issues of daily life: What's life about? What's the point of it all? Have I got it sorted? LW

Christian? This attractive booklet poses the questions: Am I a Christian? Wasn't I born one? Isn't going to church enough? What is a Christian exactly? Me in a relationship with God? LW

Who am I? A contemporary look at life, God and identity. This booklet is for young adults searching for answers to big questions. LW

Shepherds and Kings. The Christmas story told in modern language and graphics with Bible quotations – for adults or children. There are also resources on the web. LW

The Story. An innovative booklet telling the Easter story which can be read from both ends! There are also resources on the web. LW

Love is the Bridge. A small booklet incorporating John's Gospel (NIV), giving an introduction and a section at the end: 'how to know God personally'. BB

Sports booklets. High-quality outreach materials relating to international sporting tournaments such as World and European Football and the Olympic Games covering background, facts, itinerary, testimonies and an offer from Christian Enquiry Agency. CIS, DG, CPO

Game of Life. J. John relates sports to playing God's way in life and includes some spiritual exercises in this 16-page booklet. PT

It's a Wonderful Life. A booklet by J. John introducing a wonderful life with God, based on the popular film starring James Stewart. Includes photos from the film. PT

See also International Bible Society for Gospels and a good range of booklets designed for inquirers. www.eurobible.net/shop/uk/. IBSUK

Prayer cards and bookmarks for sale

A very wide range of bookmarks, prayer cards, greeting cards, posters and prints suitable for framing. Tim Tiley also produces merchandise aimed at church visitors. TT

McCrimmons are another excellent source for inspirational cards and books. A look at their website is strongly recommended. M

Cards featuring icons. St Mary's Press, Wantage, Oxon OX12 9DJ

A series of small (55 × 85 cm) brightly coloured cards illustrating Bible texts: www.eastmorn@mozcom.com

Large print materials

A range of booklets and audio materials for the blind and partially sighted is available from Torch Trust for the Blind. TTB

Posters and banners

A wide range is available from CPO.

McCrimmonds market several stunning ranges of posters that could be used both seasonally and out of season to mount displays to inform and stimulate the imagination concerning the basics of the faith. M

Attractive posters are available from TT.

Posters based on the artwork of the Benedictine Sisters and Stations of the Cross. PB&M. Also M.

Christmas posters are produced by CAN.

Resources for children

I belong to God. 'How I was baptised'. Eight-panel colour fold leaflet on thin card explaining the meaning of baptism. MU

Children and Spirituality. A4 leaflet for parents or those with care of children. MU

Josh & Jade. A series of activity sheets for 6–10 age range that introduces them to the gospel by using puzzles, codes and other activities enjoyed by children. CD

Why did Jesus come? A six-page booklet explaining what Christianity is really about and including a quiz. GBC

Re:generate. Three sets of cards and booklets for children aged 5 and over to help them talk about their feelings and their lives. LW

How is life? Booklet to help children aged 8 and over discover God's love for them. LW

Children and Bereavement. A4 guide for parents or those with care of children. MU

Waterbugs and Dragonflies. Explaining death to children. By Doris Stickney. Mowbrays 1997. ISBN 0-264-66904-5. A very helpful and inexpensive booklet to help children who are bereaved.

Be a Church Detective. A Young Person's Guide to Old Churches. By Clive Frewins. Canterbury Press 2005. ISBN 1-85311-628-9. An excellent introductory guide for children.

Cathedrals. Moonlight Publishing. First Discovery Series. ISBN 1-85103-236-3. A book for the youngest children containing wonderful transparent overlays.

Children's Bibles. IBSUK.

Display materials

A plastic rack to display free booklets and cards on a table or wall is available from LW.
A range of display racks and stands is available from TT.
A themed series of displays to introduce people to the Christian faith is available from DG.

Church security

Places of Worship Security Manual. By Nick Tolson. www.nationalchurchwatch. com

DVDs and videos

More to Life. A video and DVD magazine of a wide range of people telling their 'real life' story about how Jesus is changing their life. There's a guide on how to use this material and an associated magazine. VAV

PowerPoint presentations

A range of presentation materials and video clips is available plus other resources aimed at those who don't normally come to church. RUN

Help with projects

Andrew Drane, a corporate lawyer, is a specialist in helping churches develop cost-effective missional strategies for their buildings. Andrew Drane, Partner, Davidson Chalmers Lawyers, 12 Hope Street, Edinburgh EH2 4DB andy. drane@davidsonchalmers.com.

Useful books

Equipping your Church in a Spiritual Age. A workbook giving practical ideas to help churches engage with today's spiritual age. Group for Evangelisation. (2005) ISBN 0-8516-9314-8.
Associated books are *Evangelism in a Spiritual Age*, and *Beyond the Fringe*. ECP
Welcome to Our Church. A small illustrated handbook prepared by the Stewardship Department of the St Albans Diocese. StAD

Rural Visitors (2001) ISBN 0-9540766-0-5 and *Rural Mission* (2002) ISBN 0-9540766-1-3. Parish workbooks for the country church. Every rural church that takes its ministry to congregation and visitors seriously can profit from these helpful books. By Leslie Francis and Jeremy Martineau. ARC and CP

Open All Hours. Reordering of church buildings for community use. ISBN 0-9516871-7-4. ARC and CP

From Strangers to Pilgrims. By Richard Askew. No 48 in the Grove Evangelism Series. 1997. Thinking of the church's ministry to visitors and our witness to them of our faith. ISBN 1-85174-342-1. GB

Churches, Cathedrals and Chapels. By R. Morris and M. Corbishley. A book of particular interest to teachers. Written to help young people to focus on church architecture and furnishings. English Heritage (1996). ISBN 1-85074-447-5.

The Church Explorer's Handbook. A guide to looking at churches and their contents. By C. Fewins. 2005. ISBN 1-85311-622-X. CP and OTC

Discovering Churches. By L. Rock, Lion Publishing (1995). ISBN 0-7459-2920-6.

How to Read a Church. By R. Taylor, Rider (2003). ISBN 1-8441-3053-3.

Disability issues

CARIS. For teaching resources for churches and general information. CARIS Office, Shallowford House, Shallowford, Stone, Staffordshire ST15 0NZ.

Church Action on Disability. Co-ordinator: Martyn Pope, 50, Scrutton Street, London EC2A 4PH. 020 7452 2085.

Guild of Church Braillists. Secretary: Mrs Mabel Owen. 321 Feltham Hill Road, Ashford, Middlesex TW15 1LP.

Guild of Methodist Braillists. Hon. Gen. Secretary: Mr Colin Bringle. 19 Brookfield Road, Churchdown, Gloucester GL3 2PR.

RNIB Customer Services. Free catalogue, PO Box 173, Peterborough PE2 6WS. 0345 023 153.

RADAR. A key information point on legislation. 12 City Forum, 250 City Road, London EC1V 8AF. Information line open Monday – Friday 10 am – 4 pm. 0171 250 3222. radar@radar.org.uk.

SENSE. The National Deafblind and Rubella Association. The Princess Royal Centre, 4 Church Road, Edgbaston, Birmingham B15 3TD. 0121 456 1656.

Through the Roof. A Christian organisation that deals with disability issues. PO Box 353, Epsom, Surrey KT18 5WS. 01372 749955. Info@throughtheroof. org

The Church Among Deaf People. This is an excellent introduction to the place of deaf people within the Church. CHP

The Disability Discrimination Act: What Service Providers Need to Know. A brief guide to the Act, available free of charge from The Agenda, Freepost, London SE99 7SQ. 0345 622 633

Training for church welcomers

Welcome to the Church. A highly acclaimed course written for churches developed from the Wales Tourist Board's 'Welcome Host'. www.fsnet.co.uk/mainframe.htm

The churchyard

Wildlife in Church and Churchyard. By N. Cooper (1995). ISBN 0 7-7151-7587-4. CHP

The Churchyards Handbook 2001 (4th edn). By T. Cocke. ISBN 0-7151-7583-1. CHP

Wildlife in the Churchyard: The Plants and Animals of God's Acre. By Francesca Greenoak. Little Brown (1993). ISBN 0-856138-002.

Planting a Bible Garden. By F.N. Hepper. HMSO (1987). ISBN 0-800717-562.

The Christian Ecology Link may be of interest: www.christian-ecology.org.uk

Websites

www.highways.gov.uk/business
Your church may qualify for a brown tourist sign or for a general local sign.

www.eurobible.net/shop/uk
This is the website for the International Bible Society UK. Browsers will find a good range of gospels, children's Bibles and Bible-based material that is designed for enquirers with little or no previous knowledge.

www.rejesus.co.uk
This website exists to introduce people to Jesus, his followers and what it means to be a Christian. Churches can put www.rejesus.co.uk on literature for visitors and include a link to it from their website. There are ten ideas on the website for how to use it in evangelism.

www.life4seekers.co.uk
A website for those wishing to discover more about the Christian faith created by the Catholic Enquiry Office.

www.thegoodbookstall.org.uk
A helpful-looking site for finding resources.

www.shineonline.net
This is the Redemptorist website and will give access to a wide range of resources that could be of value.

www.caseresources.org.uk
All-embracing online resources for Catholics wishing to be involved in Evangelisation.

www.openchurchestrust.org.uk
Open Churches Trust, the creation of Lord Andrew Lloyd Webber, aims to be able to help the congregations of the finest churches to open them so the public can enjoy not only their beauty and structure but also the often unique history each can extol.

www.churchestourismassociation.info
This is a very useful site giving a wealth of information covering the whole spectrum of church tourism.

www.sloughschoolsonline.org.uk/SACRE/baptist.htm
Slough Baptist Church has developed some highly respected programmes for Year 6 school pupils based on the festivals of Christmas and Easter in co-operation with local schools.

www.qca.org.uk
Qualifications and Curriculum Authority. Downloads are available from DfES covering all religious education requirements.

www.visitchurches.org.uk
The Churches Conservation Trust website has dedicated education pages which provide booking details, suggestions for educational work, details of free tours and introductory sessions and downloadable resources such as 'Tips for busy teachers' and exemplar schemes of work for art, history and RE.